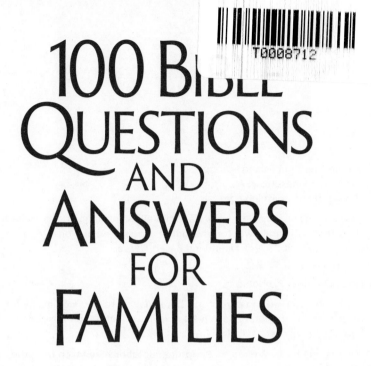

100 BIBLE QUESTIONS AND ANSWERS FOR FAMILIES

INSPIRING TRUTHS,
HELPFUL EXPLANATIONS,
AND POWER FOR LIVING
FROM GOD'S ETERNAL WORD

ALEX MCFARLAND
& BERT HARPER

BroadStreet
PUBLISHING

BroadStreet Publishing® Group, LLC
Savage, Minnesota, USA
BroadStreetPublishing.com

100 Bible Questions and Answers for Families: Inspiring Truths, Helpful Explanations, and Power for Living from God's Eternal Word
Copyright © 2023 Alex McFarland & Bert Harper

9781424566815 (softcover)
9781424566822 (ebook)

Stock or custom editions of BroadStreet Publishing titles may be purchased in bulk for educational, business, ministry, fundraising, or sales promotional use. For information, please email orders@broadstreetpublishing.com.

Cover and interior by Garborg Design Works | garborgdesign.com

Printed in China

23 24 25 26 27 5 4 3 2 1

TABLE OF CONTENTS

Section 3: Old Testament Challenges

Section 4: Questions about God

Section 5: Questions about the Holy Spirit

Section 6: Questions about Worldview

Section 7: New Testament Questions

Section 8: Questions about Jesus

Section 9: Questions about Salvation

Section 10: Questions about Marriage and Parenting

Section 11: Questions about Church and Christian Living

Section 12: Questions about the End Times

INTRODUCTION

For more than a decade, it has been our honor to host the radio program *Exploring the Word* on American Family Radio. Every weekday afternoon from three to four central time (four to five eastern time), we communicate spiritual truths and enjoy phone conversations with thousands of people who have shared challenging questions and thoughts regarding the Bible.

After we published our first book containing the top one hundred Bible questions, we were overwhelmed by the responses of the thousands of people who requested copies. Many used the book to grow in their own faith, and others shared it with friends or family members. Still others used the book as an outreach tool to discuss the gospel with those who were still uncertain of their own relationship with God.

As we considered what to do next, we quickly realized that we were unable to include dozens of other questions in our first book. We could easily add a second volume to the series to answer even more of the top questions people have asked us over the years.

Our goal for the first volume was straightforward: define the question, consider the options and evidence, and propose biblical conclusions, leaving room for preferences where the Bible does not offer a direct response. Many people greatly appreciated our attitude of sticking to Scripture, reasoning from the evidence, and offering hope and help for the real-life challenges and questions believers and unbelievers face.

Before we dive into this second volume, we want to also share a bit of perspective from our many years of addressing controversial issues as ministers and radio broadcasters. First, a question behind the question often exists. What do we mean by this? Let us share an example. Sometimes a person calls in and says they don't believe in hell. The person seems to believe what the Bible says on other topics but doesn't want to address this issue. In conversation, we often discover the true concern or questions behind the question. Usually, the caller has recently lost a loved one and does not want to consider that the person could be in hell for eternity. This is understandable, and we need to offer compassion in such cases. However, we also must direct these tough questions back to the Bible, allowing it to have authority over our emotions.

Second, fruitful questions and answers come in the context of a trusting relationship. For example, we have had the same person call into the radio show on multiple occasions. As this person has come to know us and discovered our genuine desire to help people grow spiritually, they became more open to our discussions and conclusions. This trust often takes time, with some callers telling us they have listened for years before contacting us with a question.

Third, it's okay to acknowledge gray areas or unknowns in Scripture. Yes, God knows everything. Yes, the Bible is perfect. But no, we do not know everything, and the Bible does not address every detail of life. Instead, God inspired the writers of Scripture to give us the principles we need to address today's issues. When it comes to using technology or responding to cancel culture or even handling relationships with stepchildren or blended families, we look to what the Bible does say and do our best to apply it to areas that Scripture does not directly address.

Fourth, don't forget the Holy Spirit's role. We have God's Word, but we are not God. As we address questions, we must also pray for those we serve and ask God to intervene in individual hearts and situations. Sometimes the issue is not an intellectual issue; it is a heart issue that only God can change.

We also want to impress upon you the importance of answering the tough questions of others. You may feel inadequate to address the many concerns of others, but Scripture says your efforts are vital. We love the third verse of Jude 3, which says, "Beloved, while I was very diligent to write to you concerning our common salvation, I found it necessary to write to you exhorting you to contend earnestly for the faith which was once for all delivered to the saints." Jesus' half brother wrote these words. Jude grew up with the Son of God in his home, and even he believed that it was essential to address tough questions in addition to sharing the gospel with unbelievers.

One of the best ways to share the gospel is by being strong in your own faith. The Great Commandment calls us to "love the LORD your God with all your heart, with all your soul, and with all your mind" (Matthew 22:37). We are good at teaching people to love God with their heart and soul, but we often neglect the mind. If we are to fulfill the Great Commandment, we must also be committed to loving God with our mind through growth and learning.

As we mentioned in our previous book, we have selected some of the most controversial topics of our time. You might not agree with every conclusion we give, especially regarding topics about which the Bible doesn't give a direct answer. We encourage you to be like the Bereans. Acts 17:11 says, "They received the word with all readiness, and searched the Scriptures daily to find out whether these things were so."

In addition, remember that we seek to know the truth in order to live the truth. James 1:22–25 warns, "Be doers of the word, and not hearers only, deceiving yourselves. For if anyone is a hearer of the word and not a doer, he is like a man observing his natural face in a mirror; for he observes himself, goes away, and immediately forgets what kind of man he was. But he who looks into the perfect law of liberty and continues in it, and is not a forgetful hearer but a doer of the work, this one will be blessed in what he does."

You may also notice that we have included a lot of Scripture in this book. This is intentional, as we want God's Word to serve as our authority in answering tough spiritual questions. However, we also encourage you to look up the passages in your own Bible, make notes, and meditate on the Scriptures to better know and apply them to your own life.

Finally, we also want to encourage you to communicate with us regarding how this book helps you and to ask other questions you have. You can send us a message through AlexMcFarland.com or email our *Exploring the Word* radio program at word@afa.net. We also encourage you to join us live every weekday at AFR.net or on an American Family Radio station near you. May God continue to bless your life as you explore the Word!

THE BIBLE

1. HOW LONG AGO WAS THE BIBLE WRITTEN, AND WHO WROTE IT?

The Bible is a book that consists of sixty-six works, spanning three continents, three languages, and more than fourteen hundred years of revelation. Approximately forty authors, ranging from a shepherd to kings, completed its writings. Few books of the Bible specifically name their authors, but most clearly identify the main characters or the story they would tell. While we do not have absolute proof of authorship because no original manuscripts exist, we can construct a reliable reference for the books and conclude their authorship. This dating and byline are based on the language they used and repeated in other books, on historical references to kings and nations of their time, and on the biblical characters they describe.

The Old Testament includes thirty-nine books written over the course of one thousand years between about 1400 to 400 BC. Those books were written mostly in Hebrew with some Aramaic. Moses wrote the first five books of the Bible, Genesis through Deuteronomy, by approximately 1400 BC. These books are often called the Torah or the Law.

The Historical Books (Joshua through Nehemiah) cover 1400 to 400 BC, including the history of Israel in the land of Israel and after their return to Jerusalem under Ezra and Nehemiah. The likely author of Joshua is Joshua. Judges, Ruth, and 1 and 2 Samuel are attributed to the prophets Samuel, Nathan, and Gad. Jeremiah wrote the books of 1 and 2 Kings, whereas Ezra wrote 1 and 2 Chronicles, Ezra, and Nehemiah. Mordecai is the likely author of Esther and Moses of Job.

The Poetical Books (Esther through Song of Songs) include a variety of times. Job may have been the earliest biblical book written as it references events prior to the law of Moses though its date is unknown. The Psalms mostly cover the time periods of David and Solomon (around 1000 BC) though some psalms were written as early as Moses (1400 BC) or as late as the return to Jerusalem (in the 400s BC).

The book of Proverbs was largely written during the lifetime of Solomon—and mostly by King Solomon. God had answered Solomon's request for wisdom (2 Chronicles 1:10), and as a result, Solomon was able to compose and comprise the wise sayings that make up the first twenty-five chapters of this book. Chapters 25 through 29 are also the Proverbs of Solomon, but Hezekiah's men are credited with their preservation (Proverbs 25:1). Chapter 30 is credited to one of Solomon's contemporaries, a man named Agur. Chapter 31 is credited to King Lemuel, but to give credit where it is due, the Word of God specifies that this final chapter of the book contains proverbs Lemuel learned from his mother. We know that the ultimate author of Proverbs (and all Scripture) is God himself through the Holy Spirit (see 2 Samuel 23:2; John 14:26; 2 Timothy 3:16-17; 1 Peter 1:20-21). The Triune God—whom the Bible calls "the Spirit of prophecy" (Revelation 19:10)—led Solomon to also pen Ecclesiastes and the Song of Songs.

The Prophets begin as early as the 800s BC (as was likely the case of Obadiah and Joel), and the last prophetic books (such as Malachi) were completed in the 400s. The Prophets are usually divided into the Major Prophets (Isaiah through Daniel) and the Minor Prophets (Hosea through Malachi). They are named for their main character and also their writer, much like the Gospels.

After a "silence" of approximately four centuries, the New Testament was written in twenty-seven books that cover the life of Jesus and the first generation of Christians that spanned the first century AD. The four Gospels include three books likely written in the 60s (Matthew, Mark, and Luke). Theologians usually suggest that the gospel of John was written between AD 70 and 90.

Acts was written as the second part of Luke's gospel. It covers the period from the ascension of Jesus in either AD 30 or 33 to the imprisonment of Paul in Rome in about AD 62. It was likely written in 62 or shortly afterward.

The Epistles of Paul (through Romans through Philemon) were written during his lifetime. He became a follower of Christ by AD 38, within five years of the resurrection of Jesus, and died in the mid-60s.

Hebrews is the one anonymous book of the New Testament, and it discusses events that likely took place in the AD 60s or 70s. Its mention of Timothy, the recipient of 1 and 2 Timothy, suggests a time of writing in the mid-60s to late 60s.

The Later Epistles (or General Epistles) include 1 Peter through Jude and were all likely composed during AD 60s through the 90s. The authors included Peter (who died in the 60s), the apostle John (who died by the end of the first century), and Jude (the half brother of Jesus).

Some scholars suggest the apostle John wrote Revelation either in the AD 60s or 90s. The best evidence suggests a date of around 95–96, making it the final book of the New Testament, produced by the last remaining apostle.

The books of the Bible were copied and collected by the early church, with lists of most books noted together by the second century. The modern order of today's Bible is largely based on Jerome's translation of the Bible into Latin in the fourth century.[1]

2. WHAT WERE THE ORIGINAL LANGUAGES OF THE BIBLE?

The Bible's sixty-six books were written in three different languages. The Old Testament, covering thirty-nine of the Bible's books, was mostly written in Hebrew, along with some portions in Aramaic.

The Aramaic portions of the Old Testament include Daniel 2:4–7:28 and Ezra 4:8–6:18 and 7:12–26. Both books were authored during the time when Aramaic had become a more common language among the Jewish people. Aramaic words and influences are found in many additional places in the Bible. In particular, names of people, locations, and selected words in the Old Testament often use Aramaic, as both Hebrew and Aramaic use the same alphabet and are similar in structure.

Aramaic was the commonly spoken language of the Jewish people during the earthly life of Jesus, something that many New Testament accounts reveal, though the original manuscripts of the twenty-seven books of the New Testament were all composed in Greek. For example, in Mark 5:41, Jesus told a dead girl to arise with the phrase *talitha koum*. The words mean "Little girl, get up!" (NLT) in Aramaic. *Ephphatha*, used in Mark 7:34, means "be opened." The word *abba* that Jesus often uses in the Gospels is also Aramaic, indicating that Jesus likely spoke

---

1   For further reading, we suggest *From God to Us: How We Got Our Bible* by Norman L. Geisler and William E. Nix.

Aramaic as his main language. Luke 4:17–21 also reveals Jesus reading Hebrew from the book of Isaiah in a Jewish synagogue.

The use of the Greek language in the New Testament is most likely due to its dominant role in the Roman Empire during the first century. Though Latin would later become more common, authors of the Gospels, Paul's letters, and other parts of the New Testament wrote in Greek and gave the works the widest possible audience during its original time period.

The Bible teaches that its words are inspired, but scholars take much work to evaluate the existing early copies to determine the exact wording and to translate those words into modern languages. Until the Protestant Reformation of the 1500s, most languages did not have access to Scripture in their heart language. The work of scholars during and since that time have made great strides to offer access to God's Word to many people worldwide.

Today's translations of the Bible seek to use the best manuscripts of these original language documents to provide comprehensible versions of Scripture. While many readers today likely have access to the Bible in multiple copies or versions, hundreds of languages worldwide have yet to receive even one verse of Scripture in their own language. Of the more than seven thousand languages in use today, more than eighteen hundred languages still need Bible translations started, and many others have access only to portions of Scripture in their language. Further, some tribal languages continue to exist only in an oral version without a written alphabet or symbols, revealing the need for more work to provide God's Word to "all the nations" (Matthew 28:19).

3. HOW CAN WE KNOW THE COPIES OF THE BIBLE WE HAVE ARE ACCURATE?

The original copies of the Bible's books no longer exist. How can we know that the copies we have today are accurate? The process of providing an accurate Bible translation includes a close study of the existing early manuscripts and a thorough knowledge of the ancient languages.

For the Old Testament, many of its books have copies dating to the Dead Sea Scrolls that were discovered in the last century, proving that the manuscripts were in circulation well before the earthly life of Jesus and the writings of the New Testament. Jewish scribes meticulously copied the first five books of the Bible, called the Torah, to make certain no changes were made to the text. For other parts of the Old Testament, the multiple remaining early copies allow scholars to compare any differences to help provide an accurate original language copy for translators.

For the New Testament, more than fifty-eight hundred copies of handwritten Greek manuscripts containing parts or all of its books remain available today. Textual critics and New Testament scholars have painstakingly analyzed the differences among manuscripts to help determine the likely wording of the original text in all but a few places.

Nearly all of today's modern English versions of the Bible include a team of top scholars in the biblical languages who have worked together under a careful set of guidelines to develop a careful, consistent translation for modern readers. Each version of the Bible may include its own style, but the translations are based on the same key manuscripts.

More literal translations are generally best for detailed Bible study as they use the closest possible words to the original languages. The King James Version of the Bible followed a literal approach and has remained popular for more than four centuries. Modern literal versions include the

New King James Version (NKJV), New American Standard Bible (NASB), the Christian Standard Bible (CSB), and the English Standard Versions (ESV). Additionally, a variety of less literal English versions exist. Some popular versions include the New International Version (NIV) and the New Living Translation (NLT).

Over the past generation, a concern has arisen over issues related to some translations being gender inclusive or catering to other political influences. Readers should be aware of these concerns. Details about modern influences and associated changes are usually available in the intro-duction to particular versions. In addition to reading the introduction or foreword in your Bible, we also encourage readers to note the textual comments at the bottom of the pages (especially in the New Testament).

No translation of the Bible is perfect, but today's versions are generally faithful to the original manuscripts and fulfill the Bible's command to preserve God's Word as intended. The claims of some skeptics who criticize the Bible as being intentionally changed do not stand up to the evidence of centuries of research that affirms the high degree of accuracy of the Bible. As 2 Timothy 3:16–17 teaches, "All Scripture is given by inspiration of God, and is profitable for doctrine, for reproof, for correction, for instruction in righteousness, that the man of God may be complete, thoroughly equipped for every good work."

4. WHY ARE THERE SO MANY VERSIONS OF THE BIBLE? HOW DO I KNOW WHICH VERSION TO USE?

There are various reasons behind the many English ver-sions of our Bible. Each version uses a unique translation method, with many versions offering different insights into the understanding of Scripture.

One reason for the multiple versions of the Bible we have today involves changes in the English language. The words of Scripture have not changed, but the way we use our language has changed greatly over the past five hundred years. For example, the 1611 King James Version of John 3:16 reads, "For God so loued yᵉ world, that he gaue his only begotten Sonne: that whosoeuer beleeueth in him, should not perish, but haue euerlasting life." Most of us would not understand this version today, and we certainly don't speak this way.

A second reason for different Bible translations is based on translation philosophy. In other words, some versions take the most literal approach possible, but others are mostly literal, with some versions allowing more liberty to translate words and phrases into modern equivalents. This can be good or bad, depending on how the translation is conducted. For example, the English Standard Version is mostly literal and follows the same basic approach as the King James Version in using a team of scholars for translation. On the other hand, *The Message* is one person's rendering of Scripture in modern English. Both versions may have value for comparative study, but a more literal version by a team of scholars will provide a reading closer to the original meaning of Scripture.

A third reason for multiple Bible versions is theological. For example, a particular denomination may have a preferred translation because its publishing company helped create it (such as the Southern Baptist preference for the Christian Standard Bible). This can be a positive move because it means the translation methodology is consistent with the beliefs of the denomination or publisher. On the negative side, the Bible used by the Jehovah's Witnesses, called the New World Translation, intentionally changes passages, especially those referring to various names of God, as well as John 1:1 (changing "was God" to "was a god").

How can we know which version to use? There are many ways. One important method is to read the introduction to the translation you are considering so you can understand how it was translated. Your pastor or church will also usually have a recommended version and reasons for it. Another approach is to use multiple versions and compare verses with one another when studying the Bible. This can be especially helpful when using a more literal version, like the New King James Version, with an easier-to-read version, like the New Living Translation.

We must remember that the inspired Scriptures are those written in the original languages of Hebrew, Aramaic, and Greek. Our English versions are intended to help us better understand these original languages of God's perfect, inspired Word. As Psalm 119:105 teaches, "Your word is a lamp to my feet and a light to my path." Psalm 18:30 adds, "As for God, His way is perfect; the word of the Lord is proven; He is a shield to all who trust in Him."

5. WHAT IS THE BOOK OF ENOCH? IS IT PART OF THE BIBLE?

Many people have asked about the role of the Book of Enoch, an ancient Jewish work quoted in the New Testament book of Jude. Some have even claimed the Book of Enoch, also referred to as 1 Enoch, is a "missing" part of the Bible. What is the real story of this controversial book?

The biblical character Enoch is listed in the seventh generation from Adam. In Genesis 5:24, "Enoch walked with God: and...God took him" (KJV). Enoch apparently experienced a direct departure from the earth to heaven, similar to Elijah in 2 Kings 2.

In verses 14–15 of Jude, we read, "Now Enoch, the seventh from Adam, prophesied about these men also, saying, 'Behold, the Lord comes with ten thousands of His saints, to execute judgment on all, to convict all who are ungodly among them of all their ungodly deeds which they have committed in an ungodly way, and of all the harsh things which ungodly sinners have spoken against Him.'" The verses are quoted from a document known as the Book of Enoch.

The Book of Enoch was not written by the Enoch from Genesis but was a Jewish writing that existed prior to the New Testament. It was known to many people in that time period. Fragments of this work have been found in the Dead Sea Scrolls in Hebrew and Aramaic. However, the only complete copies are in the Ethiopian language of Ge'ez. It is uncertain whether the Ethiopian version is the same as the original version.

The existing version includes 108 sections that cover "watchers," who were angel and human hybrids called Nephilim (as in Genesis 6, though it is uncertain how much real connection exists between the Genesis account and the descriptions in the Book of Enoch). The book also includes parables, information about astronomy, and various dreams, visions, and instructions.

The book is certainly not a missing book of the Bible. The Book of Enoch was written between the times of the Old and New Testaments. Instead, the case is an example of the Bible quoting from another written source as an example. However, it does not claim that the entire quoted source is inspired. The apostle Paul also quoted extrabiblical sources in the New Testament. In Acts 17:28, Luke quoted Paul, saying, "Also some of your own poets have said, 'For we are also His offspring.'" In Titus 1:12, Paul also wrote, "One of them, a prophet of their own, said, 'Cretans are always liars, evil beasts, lazy gluttons.'" He certainly did not intend for the work of a non-Christian Cretan prophet to be considered inspired Scripture.

On a related note, it is interesting that the Mormon Church considers Enoch (what they refer to as 1 Enoch) as part of its inspired writings. Portions of Enoch are included in the Mormon book of Moses though it does not include the full Ethiopic version of the book as part of its writings.

Instead of viewing the Book of Enoch as a missing book of the Bible or an inspired work, we should consider it to be similar to other ancient documents. We may use it for historical or cultural information, but we should not consider it to be equal to the Bible.

6. THE BOOK OF ENOCH CLAIMS EVE HAD SEXUAL RELATIONS WITH SATAN TO PRODUCE CAIN. IS THIS FOUND IN THE BIBLE?

The Book of Enoch mentions the world's first woman, Eve, having sexual relations with Satan and giving birth to Cain. Is this what the Bible teaches?

Definitely not! The view is part of what has been called the serpent seed doctrine. The view claims that the fall of humanity was primarily sexual, with the serpent tempting Eve to have relations with Satan. There are several reasons to debunk this view as historically and biblically inaccurate.

First, the view is not mentioned in the book of Genesis, the primary biblical account of Adam and Eve. Instead, Satan tempted Eve to eat fruit from a tree that was prohibited. She also shared the fruit with Adam, with sin entering humanity through their disobedience.

Second, the Bible specifically teaches that Cain was the son of Adam and Eve. Genesis 4:1 says, "Now Adam knew Eve his wife, and she conceived and bore Cain, and said, 'I have acquired a man from the LORD.'" Notice that the verse specifically says, "Adam knew his wife," referring to sexual relations. Cain's conception was the result of Adam and Eve's relationship.

Third, Genesis 4:1 also specifically states Cain was "from the LORD." This means Eve considered Cain a gift from God. How could Cain be a gift from God if he had been conceived by Satan?

Fourth, the rest of the Bible exclusively and repeatedly describes Cain as the son of Adam and Eve. In addition to the multiple times in Genesis that include Cain, the New Testament mentions Cain on three occasions (Hebrews 11:4; 1 John 3:12; Jude v. 11).

Fifth, the serpent seed view is based on a twisted version of Cain as being "of the wicked one," indicating he was conceived by Satan. First John 3:12 mentions Cain murdering his brother Abel, calling Cain "of the wicked one." However, the same verse adds that the reason was that "his works were evil." There was no reference to Cain being conceived by Satan.

In the eleventh verse of Jude, the author blamed wrongdoers in his time as going "the way of Cain." The reference was clearly to Cain's sinful actions regarding his unacceptable offering and the murder of his brother. Jude later quoted from the Book of Enoch (vv. 14–15) but did not describe Cain as being conceived by Satan.

Historically, some people have even used the phrase "son of Cain" to refer to those who do evil. The term has also been used as a racist statement. However, the Bible provides no basis for such teachings. Instead, Cain's disobedience serves as a warning to those who would do wrong, especially in harming others.

The serpent seed doctrine has also been associated with the interpretation of the Nephilim in Genesis 6. Some argue that the Nephilim involved fallen angels (demons) who had sexual relations with women in Noah's time. While this is one possible view, it does not have any connection with the view of Cain being the result of a relationship between Eve and Satan.

The view of Eve having relations with Satan is biblically, historically, and theologically inaccurate. The Bible describes Eve as the mother of all the living. Though imperfect, she holds an important role in Scripture and in the history of humanity.

7. WHAT DOES THE BIBLE SAY ABOUT DINOSAURS? ARE THERE DINOSAURS IN THE BIBLE?

Dinosaurs are an important part of historical study and remain a fascinating part of our culture, such as through the *Jurassic Park* and *Jurassic World* film franchises. What does the Bible teach about their existence?

First, God created dinosaurs along with all other forms of life. Genesis describes God's creation of all animals in the sea, on the land, and in the air (Genesis 1–2).

Second, the widespread, sudden deaths of many dinosaurs is consistent with the Bible's account of a global flood as described in Genesis 6–9. Other than the animals on the ark with Noah and his family, all land animals were judged with death. In Genesis 6:17, God said, "Behold, I, even I, do bring a flood of waters upon the earth, to destroy all flesh, wherein is the breath of life, from under heaven; and every thing that is in the earth shall die" (KJV). The Genesis flood may explain why large sea creatures remain even today though large species of dinosaurs no longer exist on land. Even after the flood, the rescue of animals on the ark could help explain the more recent findings of some large, dinosaur-like animals. An increasing number of modern discoveries have unearthed images and descriptions of dinosaur-like creatures in various parts of the world within the past five thousand years that may be more than legendary accounts.

Third, several verses in the Old Testament may describe various types of dinosaurs that might have existed during the times humans lived. Most of these references are in the book of Job, which many consider the earliest Old Testament book. Job 3:8 and 41:1 mention a

"Leviathan." Some describe this unknown creature as a large sea creature that could resemble an underwater dinosaur. The Leviathan is also mentioned in Psalms 74:14 and 104:25–26 and Isaiah 27:1.

The Hebrew language also includes the word *tanniyn*, which some scholars translate as "dragon" or "serpent." It is uncertain which animal the word describes, with some claiming the word could include a dinosaur. The word *tanniyn* is used in Job 7:12, which says, "Am I a sea, or a sea serpent, that You set a guard over me?" Psalm 74:13 adds, "You broke the heads of the sea serpents in the waters."

Scripture also mentions a creature traditionally referred to as the "behemoth." It is described in Job 40 as an animal that lives near water and is very strong. The description also adds that it was a plant eater, so it was unlikely a crocodile. The animal may have been a dinosaur or another now-extinct animal. If so, it offers evidence that dinosaurs may have lived in the Middle East during a period when humans could view and describe them.

Though much remains unknown about the history and extinction of dinosaurs, their existence, death, and even possible descriptions are mentioned in the words of the Bible.

SECTION 2

ALLEGED BIBLE CONTRADICTIONS

8. How could Moses have written the book of Deuteronomy if it records his death?

Moses is known as the human author of the first five books of the Old Testament from Genesis to Deuteronomy. But Deuteronomy 34 describes the death of Moses. How could Moses have written this content?

There are two main ways to handle this question. First, some have suggested that Moses wrote the last chapter before his death, predicting how his life would end. God often allowed his prophets to predict events that would take place in the future, so this explanation is possible. However, the details in the chapter seem to indicate the material was produced sometime after his death, making this an unlikely scenario.

The second way to understand the final chapter of Deuteronomy is to accept that someone else wrote it and added it at the end of the content Moses wrote. Joshua probably composed the words because he was another inspired human author of Scripture who wrote the book after Deuteronomy. Joshua was also the aide or assistant to Moses who often wrote down what Moses said. He is the most likely person to have written about the death of Moses in the account that ended Deuteronomy.

We often look at Scripture from our modern perspective in ways that may not fit the original cultural understanding of the Bible. For example, in Old Testament times, books were not mass-produced and published by companies with contracts regarding authorship. Instead, people painstakingly produced books on animal skins using handmade ink. The scroll would have been carefully guarded and transported to protect it from damage by weather and people. Multiple people were also often involved in the making of ancient books. In the case of Deuteronomy, theologians consider Moses to be the human author because he was the main person God spoke through to provide the content of the book. However, Joshua most likely wrote down the account of the death of Moses and may have been involved in other aspects of the writing of Deuteronomy.

Even today many deceased authors have had books published that another person completed. The deceased author is still considered the author even if another person is involved in completing the work. A good example is *The Silmarillion.* J. R. R. Tolkien, the bestselling author of *The Lord of the Rings*, wrote most of the book. However, his son Christopher Tolkien completed and published *The Silmarillion* after his father's death.

The Bible is both a human composition and a work inspired by God. The Lord worked through people to produce the exact words he wanted to pass down to us today. It is amazing to consider that God worked through Moses and Joshua thirty-four hundred years ago to create the words we read in our modern Bibles.

Deuteronomy was also one of the most popular books the Jews read during the time of Jesus. Jesus quoted from the book three times to thwart the deceptions of the devil when Satan tempted him in the wilderness (Matthew 4:1–11). Importantly, Jesus also referred to Moses as the author of the books of the law (Mark 10:5; 12:19–27). The gospels of Luke and John also refer to Moses as the author of the Law (Luke 20:28–38; John 1:45). Moses wrote Deuteronomy, but the book's final words were most likely written by his assistant Joshua.

9. WHY ARE THERE DIFFERENCES IN THE DETAILS AMONG THE BOOKS OF SAMUEL, KINGS, AND CHRONICLES?

The books of 1 Samuel through 2 Chronicles cover the same period of time in two different ways. The books of 1 and 2 Samuel and 1 and 2 Kings describe the history of Israel from the time of Samuel, the final judge, until Israel's deportation to Babylon and the time of King Jehoiachin. The books of 1 and 2 Chronicles, likely composed or compiled by Ezra the priest, start from the first man, Adam, through the proclamation of Jews returning to Israel from Babylon.

Despite covering the same basic events, the books also include various differences in details. The books of Samuel and Kings emphasize the highlights, good and bad, of the various leaders of Israel, including the kings of both the Northern Kingdom of Israel and the Southern Kingdom of Judah during the divided kingdom.

The books of Chronicles emphasize the history of the Jewish people. They begin with Adam, offering a genealogy up until the time of King David. The books of Chronicles emphasize David's kingdom and his descendants, especially the kings of Judah, who followed God's ways more often than the kings of Israel. The kingdom of Judah eventually fell into judgment as well, with the fall of Jerusalem and the deportation of Jews to Babylon occurring near the end of 2 Chronicles. The book ends on a note of hope as

God's people receive permission to return to Jerusalem and rebuild the temple after seventy years in captivity.

Beyond the differences in themes, some skeptics have been critical of differences in some details between the books of Samuel and Kings and the books of Chronicles. For example, 1 and 2 Chronicles highlight David and Solomon in mostly positive ways, but 1 and 2 Samuel and 1 and 2 Kings reveal more about the failings of the two early Jewish kings. Why the differences?

The main issue, again, is the writers' purpose and emphasis. The books of Samuel and Kings emphasize the good and bad of each king in the history of Israel, whereas the books of Chronicles focus more on the story of the Jewish people. David and Solomon were largely defined as key leaders in God's story for his people rather than defined by their sinful failings.

Some have suggested the books of Chronicles were written after the books of Samuel and Kings and therefore did not need to duplicate some of the negative accounts regarding David, Solomon, or other Jewish leaders. The date of their writing is uncertain, though if Ezra wrote 1 and 2 Chronicles, he would have done so after 1 and 2 Samuel and 1 and 2 Kings were written.

When it comes to details, the differences are also small and not necessarily contradictory as some have claimed. For example, in 2 Samuel 7:16, Nathan said, "Your house and your kingdom shall be established forever before you. Your throne shall be established forever." In 1 Chronicles 17:14, Nathan said, "I will establish him in My house and in My kingdom forever; and his throne shall be established forever." Which is correct? Skeptics claim both cannot be right.

A close comparison of the verses, even in the original language of Hebrew, shows that the wording is only slightly different. The author of the later work (likely Ezra in 1 Chronicles) did not attempt to cite the words exactly. Citation in ancient times was also not as exact as today. The original audience would not have read the two versions and claimed that any contradiction had taken place. The essential message remains unchanged in both places.

In summary, the books of Samuel, Kings, and Chronicles cover the same time period and many of the same events, but each book has its own themes that present the material in the way God intended to help us know him and grow in him today. These works are vital to understanding the long history of the Lord's plan for the Jewish people as well as how he has worked over the centuries to keep his promises.

10. HOW COULD GOD BE "SORRY" (GENESIS 6:6) THAT HE MADE PEOPLE AFTER MAKING THEM IN HIS IMAGE?

In Genesis 6:6, we read, "The LORD was sorry that He had made man on the earth, and He was grieved in His heart." How could God be sorry that he made people? What does this mean?

The larger context of the passage is the key to understanding this verse. Verse 5 says, "Then the LORD saw that the wickedness of man was great in the earth, and that every intent of the thoughts of his heart was only evil continually." The emphasis was on God's anger over the sins of his people. God was not simply sorry that he had made people on the earth. He was disappointed or upset over how humanity had turned out since the time he had created people. The passage notes in verse 7 that the Lord would destroy all people in judgment. Verse 8 then highlights Noah, a person who "found grace in the eyes of the LORD." Verse 9 adds that Noah was "a just man, perfect in his generations. Noah walked with God." Noah was not perfect in the sense that he had never sinned. Instead, he was perfect in the sense of being mature. His relationship with God provided salvation, foreshadowing the salvation we receive in our relationship with Jesus Christ today (John 1:12; 3:16).

Verses 11–12 return to the corruption of humans. Because the earth had become "corrupt" and "filled with violence," the Lord judged the world with a flood while rescuing Noah and his family in a new beginning for humanity.

Another important aspect of this account is the literary device of giving God emotions. The Lord is not human and does not grow tired or experience similar human concerns. However, the Bible often attributes human feelings to God to help explain his actions. The Bible also describes him with human terms like "the hand of God" or the "voice of the Lord." Isaiah 55:9 teaches, "As the heavens are higher than the earth, so are My ways higher than your ways, and My thoughts than your thoughts," which means we could never truly understand God's ways or thoughts. Therefore, the writers describe God the Father as being similar to humans for our benefit to help explain his ways for our understanding.

In addition to these factors, we must remember that God knew in advance that people would become corrupt and sinful. He knew before the foundations of the universe that he would one day need to call Noah to build an ark to save his family and animal life as part of the story of redemption.

God may have been sorry about the actions of humans, but he still created them in his image, and he deeply loves them. We are also created in his image but are fallen and stand in need of the Lord's salvation to escape eternal judgment. We cannot find our salvation in an ark of wood but in the Christ who died on the wooden cross, rose from the dead, and offers us eternal life (Romans 10:9–10).

11. DID JESUS CAST DEMONS OUT OF ONE MAN OR TWO MEN (MATTHEW 8:28–33; MARK 5:1–16; LUKE 8:26–39)?

Matthew 8:28–34 and Mark 5:1–20 describe Jesus sending away a demon from two men, but Luke 8:26–39 includes only one man. Why are there differences between these accounts?

The timing of the account clearly describes the same event. Jesus had just calmed a storm prior to landing at the location where the actions occurred. Luke's mention of only one man does not necessarily mean that a second person was not involved. He may have simply chosen to emphasize the experience of one of the men. Though a reason for doing so is not specifically given, Luke's emphasis on the one man freed from demons appears to highlight certain aspects of the account that show the power of Jesus and how his work in the lives of unlikely people can lead to a tremendous transformation.

First, the man that Luke discussed revealed his name was Legion, a word referring to the many demons within him. A Roman military legion could include up to six thousand soldiers, though in the context of Luke's account, it likely only indicated a large, unspecified number of evil spirits at work within the man.

Second, the evil spirits were powerful enough to enter and kill an entire herd of pigs (Luke 8:32–33). Again, Luke gives no specific number of pigs, but the herd could have included hundreds of pigs, offering a violent image for Luke's early readers.

Third, the scene reveals that Jesus could simply speak the word and a multitude of demons would flee. They were powerful enough to kill many animals but not powerful enough to resist the Messiah.

Fourth, the account shows the value of the demon-possessed man. His life was worth more than a herd of pigs, despite his despised status by the people of his community. The account is an illustration of Jesus' teaching that we are worth more than many sparrows (Matthew 10:31).

Fifth, Luke 8:38 says, "Now the man from whom the demons had departed begged Him that he might be with Him." Jesus had transformed him. Now he wanted to stay with Jesus. The healed man's response was in strong contrast to the people of the village. Verse 37 says "the whole multitude" asked Jesus to leave. They were afraid of him. The healed man no longer lived in fear. He had experienced a faith in Jesus that made him want to be with the Lord and tell others about him. Rather than allowing the man to accompany him, Jesus told him in verse 39, "Return to your own house, and tell what great things God has done for you." The account ends by revealing that the man "went his way and proclaimed throughout the whole city what great things Jesus had done for him."

12. WHY DOES THE BIBLE SAY GOD CHANGED HIS MIND BUT ALSO SAYS GOD DOES NOT CHANGE HIS MIND?

The Bible teaches that God is perfect. Therefore, he should not need to change his mind. But there are places in Scripture that seem to indicate God has changed his mind, like when God decided not to destroy Nineveh after Jonah preached and the people repented. Does God change his mind or not?

Malachi 3:6 is clear that God does not change his mind: "I am the Lord, I change not" (KJV). Numbers 23:19 adds, "God is not a man, that He should lie, nor a son of man, that He should repent. Has He said, and will He not do? Or has He spoken, and will He not make it good?"

God also clearly knows all things and has no need to change his mind. He knows the end from the beginning, made all things, and controls all things. God said in Isaiah 46:9–10, "Remember the former things of old, for I am God, and there is no other; I am God, and there is none like Me, declaring the end from the beginning, and from ancient times things that are not yet done." Ezekiel also confirms God's knowledge of all things and his unchanging plan. "I the Lᴏʀᴅ have spoken it: it shall come to pass, and I will do it" (24:14 KJV).

But how do we explain times when God seems to change due to various circumstances in Scripture? To better understand these accounts, it is important to remember the way Scripture uses human emotions or expressions to explain God's actions. This sometimes happens in relation to human body parts ascribed to God though he is not a human. The Bible refers to the arm of the Lord though God the Father does not have arms in the same way people have arms. The same is true of our human emotions. The Bible may refer to God being sad or happy or even to God changing his mind, but the biblical writers were simply expressing God's unfolding plan in ways that our human minds can grasp. We certainly cannot fully understand how God knew everything from beginning to end before he made the universe, but we can identify with God not bringing judgment on the city of Nineveh after they humbled themselves before him.

Another revealing example is in John 6 when Jesus feeds the five thousand. He asked Philip where they could buy bread for all the people. In verse 6, John revealed, "This [Jesus] said to test him, for He Himself knew what He would do." The apostle Andrew also doubted. He said, "There is a lad here who has five barley loaves and two small fish, but what are they among so many?" (v. 9). Yet the account concluded with twelve baskets of food left after everyone finished eating. This happened to be enough for each disciple to carry a basket. Could Jesus be any clearer regarding his testing of their faith?

Jesus knew he was about to perform a miracle to feed the people, yet he still asked his disciple a question as part of his plan to help Philip grow. God certainly still does similar work today in our lives. We may feel like God changes his mind on us at times, but he already knows his plan for our lives. He may be seeking to help us grow in new ways. Instead of doubting him, we can use such times to deepen our trust in him, knowing he is the never-changing God, perfect in all his ways.

13. Why does Jesus say we should "hate" our father and mother (Luke 14:26) when one of the Ten Commandments teaches us to honor our parents?

Why did Jesus teach that we should hate our father and mother? Doesn't this contradict one of the Ten Commandments that teaches we are to honor our parents?

Jesus certainly affirmed honoring our parents. He specifically challenged the religious leaders of his time who set aside the command to honor their parents to serve God (Mark 7:9–13). But we also read in Luke 14:26, "If anyone comes to Me and does not hate his father and mother, wife and children, brothers and sisters, yes, and his own life also, he cannot be My disciple." The context of this teaching focuses on leaving everything to follow Jesus. He taught that following him must come before parents, spouse, children, siblings, and even our own life.

Jesus then gave two examples to emphasize his teaching. First, he used the illustration of building a tower in verses 28–30: "Which of you, intending to build a tower, does not sit down first and count the cost, whether he has enough to finish it—lest, after he has laid the foundation, and is not able to finish, all who see it begin to mock him, saying, 'This man began to build and was not able to finish'?" The focus of this example was on counting the cost involved in the project before committing to it.

The second example included a king going to war in verses 31–32: "What king, going to make war against another king, does not sit down first and consider whether he is able with ten thousand to meet him who comes against him with twenty thousand? Or else, while the other is still a great way off, he sends a delegation and asks conditions of peace." Jesus emphasized planning ahead before committing to a life-changing decision.

The Lord concluded the account with the words, "Whoever of you does not forsake all that he has cannot be My disciple" (v. 33). This includes our parents. We are to honor our parents and love them, but we are not to put our parents before the Lord.

In Luke 9:59, one potential follower of Jesus asked if he could first go and bury his father. It is unclear if the father had already passed away or was only near the end of his life. In either case, the appeal sounded noble, but Jesus spoke against the man's request. Jesus answered in verse 60, "Let the dead bury their own dead, but you go and preach the kingdom of God." Serving the Lord is more important than any other area of life, including our parents. This was what Jesus emphasized. He was not against honoring our parents but was clear that the Lord must come first in our lives.

This is a powerful reminder for those who are close to their parents or other family members who may encourage them to do things that are "good" but may not be God's plan for their future. We've spoken with many young people who have had to make difficult choices when their parents have encouraged them to take a certain career path rather than wanting their children to serve the Lord in ministry, mission work, or simply another field in which the children believe God has called them to work.

In other cases, parents mean well by desiring to keep their children from moving to another place, but God calls us to make disciples of all nations, which will sometimes require going far from home to help others find their heavenly home. It's also a strong reminder for those of us who are parents and grandparents that we must teach our children and grandchildren to follow the Lord, even when it includes difficult choices.

14. DID JESUS CARRY HIS OWN CROSS, OR DID SIMON CARRY IT FOR HIM?

Did Jesus carry his cross, or did someone else? The Bible seems to indicate both, but how can this be right? If one of the Gospels says Jesus carried his cross and another of the Gospels says someone else did, isn't that a contradiction?

A look at the four Gospels reveals the full picture. Matthew, Mark, and Luke all indicate a man named Simon from Cyrene (modern Libya) carried the cross of Jesus (Matthew 27:31–32; Mark 15:20–21; Luke 23:26). John 19:17 says, "He, bearing His cross, went out to a place called the Place of a Skull, which is called in Hebrew, Golgotha."

The writers may seem to contradict one another, but John chose to instead describe a different part of the account. Jesus had just been handed over for crucifixion after the Jewish religious leaders had argued with Pilate to sentence Jesus to death (John 19:5–16). John then shifted to Jesus with the cross and the crucifixion, describing little about the process of Jesus leaving the presence of Pilate and traveling to Golgotha outside of the city wall.

Matthew, Mark, and Luke all add details regarding Jesus leaving the presence of Pilate and walking to the place of his crucifixion. Matthew 27:31–32 reads, "When they had mocked Him, they took the robe off Him, put His own clothes on Him, and led Him away to be crucified. Now as they came out, they found a man of Cyrene, Simon by name. Him they compelled to bear His cross." The process included Jesus being mocked, the purple robe removed, his clothing returned, and Jesus being forced to walk with the crossbeam of the cross on his shoulders. Somewhere during this walk, Roman soldiers forced the man of Cyrene to help carry the cross for Jesus. Jesus was likely too weak to carry the cross the entire way. As the Roman soldiers noticed this, they would have forced a person along the road to carry it rather than perform the task themselves.

Several details are also given concerning Simon. He was most likely a Jew from Cyrene who had come to Jerusalem to observe Passover. However, he had a name common to Jews and gentiles. He was also an outsider or foreigner traveling from Africa, representing an aspect of early Christianity important in the African tradition. Simon was the father of two sons named Alexander and Rufus, who were likely with him when he was forced to carry the cross of Jesus. Mark 15:21 adds, "They compelled a passer-by coming from the country, Simon of Cyrene (the father of Alexander and Rufus), to carry His cross" (NASB).

Yet the story of Simon and his sons doesn't end at the cross. Believers from Cyrene were mentioned at the day of Pentecost (Acts 2:10) and may have included Simon and his two sons. Believers from Cyrene also fled Jerusalem after the death of Stephen (Acts 7) and may have included these men. Lucius of Cyrene was a teacher in the early church at Antioch (Acts 13:1) though it is unclear if he had any connection with Simon or his sons. Romans 16:13 also mentions a man named Rufus who was "chosen in the Lord" and lived in Rome as a believer during the time Paul wrote to the Roman Christians in the mid-50s. Some believe this is the same Rufus mentioned in Mark's gospel because the gospel of Mark is often considered a writing based on the teachings of the apostle Peter. Mark and Peter also both served in Rome in the 60s (1 Peter 5:13).

In summary, it is clear Jesus walked with his cross and that Simon later took over to carry it for him. Simon was likely a known early believer, along with his sons, and they were mentioned in the Gospels as an important part of early Christian history and as eyewitnesses of the crucifixion of Jesus.

OLD TESTAMENT CHALLENGES

15. HOW WERE THERE "DAYS" BEFORE THE FOURTH DAY OF CREATION WHEN GOD CREATED THE SUN AND MOON?

The Bible describes the creation of the universe, our planet, plant life, animal life, and humans in six days, but how were there days before the creation of the sun on the fourth day?

Theologians and Bible scholars have considered this question since ancient times, and they have answered it in a variety of ways. One answer involves understanding the definition of the word *day* in Hebrew. The word *yom* that is translated "day" can also be translated as a longer period of time. Some have used this to determine that the creation days were longer than twenty-four-hour periods. We can see the weakness of this view in other passages of the Bible that refer to creation. For example, in Exodus 20:11 (also 31:17), we read, "In six days the LORD made heaven and earth, the sea, and all that in them is, and rested the seventh day" (KJV). Moses also wrote Genesis, seeming to indicate that the days of creation were six solar days.

Another view is that God created the sun on the first day, but it did not appear as visible to the earth until the fourth day. The idea is that the description in Genesis 1 refers to the sun, moon, and stars existing earlier but not being revealed to the earth until this time. The problem with this view is that Genesis 1:16–18 specifically states God "made" the sun and moon on the fourth day: "God made two great lights; the greater light to rule the day, and the lesser light to rule the night: he made the stars also. And God set them in the firmament of the heaven to give light upon the earth, and to rule over the day and over the night, and to divide the light from the darkness" (KJV). It seems to be a stretch to claim the sun and moon already existed and simply appeared on a later day.

Some have also suggested that God is light and did not need the sun and moon for the first three days. While God can certainly do as he pleases, no evidence supports this view as the best answer for the first three days of creation.

The theologian Augustine had perhaps the best view. He admitted that there is a mystery regarding the first three days of creation. From a human standpoint, we cannot comprehend how days could be measured without the sun and moon, but God revealed that he made the sun and moon on the fourth day. He either had unknown periods of time in mind for the first three days or kept track of time without the sun and moon in a way possible only to God.

When it comes to the creation of the universe, we may not be able to fully understand all the details, but we can know the Creator who made it. In Ecclesiastes 8:17, King Solomon noted, "For though a man labors to discover it, yet he will not find it; moreover, though a wise man attempts to know it, he will not be able to find it." There is value in seeking to understand the creation of our world, but we must be humble enough to recognize there is much that is beyond our understanding.

16. HOW OLD IS THE UNIVERSE ACCORDING TO THE BIBLE?

One of the great concerns regarding faith is the age of the universe. The Bible seems to indicate the universe is young, whereas science says it has existed for more than thirteen billion years. What does the Bible really say?

The Jewish tradition is interesting in this regard. It considers 3761 BC the starting point of the world based on the genealogies of the Old Testament. From September 2023 to September 2024 is the year 5784 on the Jewish calendar.

Many Christians take a more nuanced approach that admits that some of the family records in the Old Testament were not strictly father-son, especially those listed in the Table of Nations in Genesis 10 after the Noahic flood. Giving space for multiple generations in the time between Noah and Abraham, researchers have estimated a human history of perhaps between ten thousand and twenty thousand years. These dates also better account for many of the findings of modern archaeology. For example, Native Americans have been documented in the Americas for more than six thousand years, not to mention early people in other parts of the world. These findings do not contradict a young earth creationism view of the Bible.

Some Christians have sought to reconcile modern science by accepting old earth creationism or theistic evolution. Old earth creationism (sometimes called day-age theory) believes the days of creation refer to long periods of time. While a growing number of evangelicals hold this view, it is not our belief that this is what the Bible teaches.

Theistic evolution takes another jump and proposes that the biblical account of creation is consistent with Darwinian evolutionary theory. One variation of this view, the BioLogos perspective, seeks to harmonize Scripture and evolution: "We believe that the diversity and inter-relation of all life on earth are best explained by the

God-ordained process of evolution with common descent. Thus, evolution is not in opposition to God, but a means by which God providentially achieves his purposes. Therefore, we reject ideologies that claim that evolution is a purposeless process or that evolution replaces God."[2] While the group's effort to find consistency between the Bible and science is admirable, this view assumes evolution is consistent with the Genesis account despite Scripture clearly teaching that God made plant, animal, and human life suddenly and miraculously.

In addition to these views, most modern scientists suggest that the latest data refers to our universe being 13.7 to 13.8 billion years old. This is largely based on evidence from astronomy since the launching of the Hubble telescope, which provides data that scientists use to estimate the age of our known universe.

Those who accept the Bible as God's Word have responded in a variety of ways to this data. First, some suggest that God made our universe with the appearance of age. The weakness of this view is that the scientific evidence to prove the mere appearance of age is lacking. It is a faith view rather than a scientifically based view that can be evaluated.

A second, more likely, response is that modern calculation is based on a steady rate of expansion of the universe. What does this mean? The estimation that the universe is over thirteen billion years old is based on a calculation of the universe expanding at a consistent rate over a long period of time. However, it is not certain that the universe has always expanded at the same rate.

The James Webb Space Telescope, launched in 2022, has reached farther into space and is already providing discoveries that are causing astronomers to reconsider

---

2   "What We Believe," BioLogos, accessed January 11, 2023, https://biologos.org/about-us/what-we-believe/.

previous theories regarding the beginning of the universe. The more information we discover, however, the more it appears to point to a supernatural creator who made all things in a complex manner.

Doesn't this point to the loving and powerful God of the Bible? While we may never know the exact date when God created the universe, we can see God's handiwork in its making and in sustaining it at every step in the process. The universe and our world, according to Scripture, appear to have been made in six days just thousands of years ago, in ways that the world's greatest researchers continue to seek to comprehend.

17. WHY DID SOME MEN HAVE MORE THAN ONE WIFE IN THE OLD TESTAMENT?

The Bible clearly teaches that God's creation of marriage is intended for one man and one woman in lifelong commitment (Genesis 2:24), so why did some men have more than one wife in the Old Testament?

The first person the Bible notes as having two wives is Lamech. In Genesis 4:19, we read, "Lamech took unto him two wives: the name of the one was Adah, and the name of the other Zillah" (KJV). A close look at Lamech reveals that he was not a great guy. In verse 23, he admitted that he had murdered another man. He is certainly not an example of the type of godly person we are called to follow.

But there are other examples as well. Jacob was married to both Leah and Rachel in arranged marriages after Laban deceived him. The marriages were not God's ideal, but God used them as part of his plan to bless Abraham's descendants and begin to build the nation of the Jewish people.

In 1 Samuel 1, Elkanah had two wives, including Hannah, the mother of the prophet Samuel. A reading of the passage reveals her difficult life, which included Hannah's infertility and a rivalry between the two wives.

David and Solomon are the two top examples of men who had multiple wives in the Bible. In both cases, the practice led to major problems. In the life of David, he had multiple wives on his journey to becoming king. However, he was also involved in an affair that led him to set up the woman's husband for death, and David suffered great judgment as a result.

Solomon, David's son, became king and used his position to accumulate seven hundred wives and three hundred concubines as part of his massive family (1 Kings 11:3). While people in power often had multiple wives to create more children or build alliances with other nations, Solomon's wives also led to his unfaithfulness to the Lord.

A close look at the examples of men in the Bible who married more than one woman at a time reveals that the consequences were not good. Additionally, it was never God's design for marriage to include combinations other than one man and one woman. Even divorce came about because of the Jewish people having a "hardness of [their] hearts," according to Jesus (Matthew 19:8).

In the New Testament, polygamy did not receive the same attention. In the first century, the practice was largely already prohibited. However, 1 Timothy 3 and Titus 1 require elders in the church to be the husband of only one wife. The Greek word used in these passages literally means "one-woman man," so it is unclear whether these passages specifically address polygamy or only faithful marriage, but again they affirm the importance of God's design for marriage and family.

The issue in the Bible of a man with more than one wife at a time is a good example of Scripture describing a practice versus prescribing a practice. The Old Testament often noted men with multiple wives, but it did not teach that godly people should live that way. Instead, God provided his divine design for marriage with the account of

Adam and Eve in the garden of Eden. Jesus affirmed this design for marriage, and it remains the biblical pattern for those who seek to faithfully follow the Lord today.

18. WHY DID GOD COMMAND THE ISRAELITES TO KILL ALL THE PEOPLE OF SOME TOWNS? DOES THAT MEAN GOD APPROVES OF GENOCIDE?

God commanded the Israelites to kill all the people in some of the towns they fought in the wilderness and in taking the promised land. Why did the Lord command these actions? Does God approve of genocide?

We must consider some factors from the context of these biblical passages to answer the question. First, the Israelite army was serving during a time of war. These nations were not seeking to make peace with them but seeking to kill the Jewish people. Fighting against their enemies was not optional but was a matter of self-defense.

Second, the complete destruction of Israel's enemies was largely due to keeping survivors from later attacking the Jewish people. Revenge ran deep in these cultures. If even a small number of people survived, Israel would one day face them again in battles that would take more lives.

Third, God had given these nations hundreds of years to repent, yet they had not. It was not as if God had given violent commands for the Israelite military to wipe out entire unsuspecting towns. These commands came after generations of allowing people time to change their ways.

Fourth, the Lord chose to spare those who turned to him even when they came from these ungodly cultures. A great example of this is Rahab in Joshua 2. The Israelites were instructed to kill all the people of Jericho, but God spared Rahab and her family because she helped the Jewish spies and believed in their God. The Gibeonites in Joshua 9 offer another example of God sparing an entire group of people. The Gibeonites tricked the Israelites into a treaty by acting like they were from a land far away. They became servants to Israel instead. Why? Because they feared the Lord and sought to protect themselves.

Fifth, we must remember these commands were intended for one series of battles in history and are not the norm of God's actions. Our God is full of mercy and grace, as we see throughout Scripture. However, he is also a God of judgment, which we recognize in the destruction of ungodly people at the hands of the Israelite army.

The Israelites would also receive judgment later in history for turning away from the Lord. God was not only against the people who opposed Israel during the conquest of their promised land but also against evil among his own people.

Still today, these accounts remind us of both God's love and his wrath. In our time, we have the opportunity to experience salvation through Jesus Christ (John 3:16; Ephesians 2:8–9). If we reject him, we will instead experience eternal judgment separated from God in hell.

19. HOW COULD KING DAVID BE A MAN AFTER GOD'S OWN HEART EVEN THOUGH HE COMMITTED ADULTERY?

The Bible calls David a man after God's own heart, but how can this be true if David committed adultery that included a cover-up that resulted in the death of the woman's husband?

Scripture does include a clear disclaimer against David's sinful actions. In 1 Kings 15:5, we read, "David did what was right in the eyes of the LORD, and had not turned aside from anything that He commanded him all the days of his life, except in the matter of Uriah the Hittite."

David slept with Bathsheba, the wife of Uriah. Bathsheba soon notified David that she was pregnant. David sought to cover up his sin by bringing Uriah back from war to sleep with Bathsheba so that the child would appear to be Uriah's. Instead, Uriah stayed with his soldiers. Next, David sent Uriah to the front lines of battle to intentionally kill him. He then married Bathsheba and thought his plan was complete.

The prophet Nathan later confronted David regarding his sin. David repented, and God forgave him. "David said to Nathan, 'I have sinned against the LORD.' And Nathan said to David, 'The LORD also has put away your sin; you shall not die'" (2 Samuel 12:13).

Despite David's confession and God's forgiveness, the great king of Israel would face difficult consequences in the days to follow. The child born to Bathsheba died (2 Samuel 12:18). David's other sons sought to overthrow his kingdom. His sin led to much pain for him and for his nation.

Psalm 51 shares the response of David after Nathan confronted him. Verse 10 says, "Create in me a clean heart, O God, and renew a steadfast spirit within me." David turned away from his sin and returned to walking closely with God. In verse 17, David added, "The sacrifices of God are a broken spirit, a broken and a contrite heart—these, O God, You will not despise." He recognized that the Lord would accept him if he repented and sought God's forgiveness.

The same God who forgave David forgives believers who stumble today. We can still be a person after God's own heart even after we have sinned—if we humble ourselves and turn from our wrongs. In Acts 13:22, written one thousand years after David's life, the Jewish people still remembered their former king as a godly man: "He raised up for them David as king, to whom also He gave testimony and said, 'I have found David the son of Jesse, a man after My own heart, who will do all My will.'" When we turn to the Lord and live devoted to him, we have the potential to change how God and others know us, becoming people after God's own heart, who worship him and share his love with those around us.

20. IS THE STORY OF JONAH AND THE BIG FISH A LITERAL STORY?

The account of Jonah being in the belly of a great fish for three days seems so unrealistic to some people that many have asked whether it is a literal story. Is the story a "fish tale," or did Jonah really survive three days inside a large fish? What is the evidence that the account is literal?

There was clearly no video of Jonah's survival, but there are some important factors to consider. Of great importance is that Jesus referred to Jonah's account as a literal event. In Matthew 12:40–41, he said, "For as Jonah was three days and three nights in the belly of the great fish, so will the Son of Man be three days and three nights in the heart of the earth. The men of Nineveh will rise up in the judgment with this generation and condemn it, because they repented at the preaching of Jonah; and indeed a greater than Jonah is here." If Jesus is God and his Word is true, that is all we should need in order to accept the literal, miraculous Jonah account as believers.

Archaeological discoveries in Israel have uncovered some interesting bits of evidence about the story of Jonah. For example, a first-century ossuary (bone box) found in Israel includes a sketch of Jonah being spit out by a large fish. This evidence indicates that the account was circulated and was well-known by the time the New Testament was written.[3]

In addition, a copy of the book of Jonah was found among the Dead Sea Scrolls. These scrolls date from the third century BC to the first century AD. The book of

---

3 Sebastian Kettley, "Bible News: Evidence of Jonah and the Whale Found in Jerusalem, Claims Scripture Expert," Express.co.uk, August 15, 2020, https://www.express.co.uk/news/weird/1322018/Bible-news-Jonah-and-whale-evidence-Jerusalem-archaeology.

Jonah was likely written between 793 and 758 BC, with the account widely circulating.

Another interesting piece of history related to the account is the tomb of Jonah. The Islamic State destroyed the tomb in ancient Nineveh in 2014, but Jews, Christians, and many Muslims revered the site for centuries as the historic location of Jonah's death.

Why would so many consider Jonah's tomb to be so remarkable? Even if the location is not authentic, the Old Testament book bearing Jonah's name and centering on the account of the great fish swallowing the prophet is the only way to explain logically the association of Jonah with Nineveh.

Other tales exist of a person being swallowed by a whale and surviving. But even modern accounts are often met with skepticism. Practically speaking, the Bible does not specify that the fish that swallowed Jonah was a whale. The event could have included a fish that is now extinct. Some have also suggested that the great fish was a sperm whale since a large one can swallow other fish the size of a human or larger.

The account is clearly miraculous, but that does not mean it is impossible. The Bible is filled with examples of God working through supernatural acts to accomplish his will. The account of Jonah surviving inside of a large fish for three days is one of the most vivid accounts in Scripture. Jesus specifically referred to it, and the story remains important to believers today.

21. WHY DID GOD TELL THE PROPHET HOSEA TO MARRY A PROSTITUTE?

Hosea, the first book of the Minor Prophets, begins with God commanding the prophet Hosea to marry a prostitute named Gomer. Why would God ask a godly man to marry a woman who was unfaithful to him?

The text is somewhat unclear regarding the timing of his wife's prostitution. Some believe she was a prostitute before Hosea married her. Others see the account as a prediction of his wife's prostitution, which later occurred. Hosea 3:1–3 reveals that when Hosea was married to Gomer, she ran away and was unfaithful to him. Hosea 3:2 says he purchased her back from slavery for fifteen shekels of silver and one and a half homers of barley.

God then used the tragic love story as an illustration of Israel's future. "For the children of Israel shall abide many days without king or prince, without sacrifice or sacred pillar, without ephod or teraphim. Afterward the children of Israel shall return and seek the Lord their God and David their king. They shall fear the Lord and His goodness in the latter days" (Hosea 3:4–5).

The Lord clearly used the account of Hosea and Gomer as an example of God's love for the people of Israel. They had been "married" to the Lord but had run away and "prostituted" themselves through immoral living and serving other gods. The Lord would purchase them back and make them his people once again.

From the Jewish perspective, the story was unthinkable. Why would a godly man purchase back his unfaithful wife who had been with other men? In Deuteronomy 24:1–4, the law of Moses says a woman who has been divorced could not become the wife of another man and then later return to her first husband. In Hosea's case, they were not divorced, but she had been unfaithful. Hosea had the legal right to divorce her under Jewish law. In fact, she could have been punished by death for her actions (Leviticus 20:10; Deuteronomy 22:20–24). Instead of enforcing the law, Hosea followed God's command to forgive his wife and redeem her. He took her back and made her his wife once again.

The picture was a strong one for the people of Hosea's time and remains powerful for us still today. Like Gomer, we have been unfaithful to the Lord and deserve judgment. Like Hosea, the Lord extends his mercy and forgiveness to us. Romans 8:1 says, "There is therefore now no condemnation to those who are in Christ Jesus, who do not walk according to the flesh, but according to the Spirit." Jesus gave his life on the cross and rose again "that the body of sin might be done away with, that we should no longer be slaves of sin" (Romans 6:6). The apostle Paul taught that our goal as followers of Jesus is clear. "Just as you presented your members as slaves of uncleanness, and of lawlessness leading to more lawlessness, so now present your members as slaves of righteousness for holiness" (Romans 6:19). We have been freed from the slavery of sin. We should now faithfully serve the Lord in response to his great love for us.

22. IF GOD LOVES EVERYONE, HOW CAN HE SAY, "ESAU I HAVE HATED" (MALACHI 1:3)?

In Malachi 1:3, God says he hated Esau. How can God hate Esau, or anyone else, if the Bible tells us that God loves everyone?

It is clear from other places in Scripture that God loves every person. For example, the well-known verse John 3:16 says, "God so loved the world." God's love for every person is clear and is so important that Jesus came to die to provide salvation for everyone who believes. But why does the Bible say God hated Esau?

The context of Malachi offers some insight into this alleged contradiction. Verse 2 notes that Esau and Jacob were brothers, but God blessed Jacob, and Esau did not experience the same blessings. Verse 4 speaks of Edom, the descendants of Esau, noting their struggles during Malachi's time.

The contrast reveals the book's emphasis. The Lord chose Israel to receive the blessings he promised to Abraham through his son Isaac and his grandson Jacob. God did not choose Esau, and in comparison, Esau was despised and hated. Malachi's message continues to highlight Israel's role as being favored by God though the Jewish people often disobeyed the Lord's commands.

While this contrast provides part of the answer, why does Malachi use "hate" to explain the differences between the blessing to Jacob's descendants and no blessing for Esau's descendants? The biblical writers often attributed human emotions to God's actions. When Malachi uses the word *hate*, he is using it to explain God's treatment toward Esau and the Edomites in contrast with the "love" or favor God showed to Jacob. God did not hate Esau as an individual or Esau's descendants. Instead, the plight of the Edomites and the difficult situation the Edomites faced at the time of the book's writing *appeared* to be the result of hatred. God even added in verse 4 that the Edomites might try to rebuild, but God was against them due to their disobedience.

Despite the strong wording about hatred, God still blessed Esau. In Genesis 33:9, Esau even tried to turn down his brother Jacob's gifts, claiming he already had enough. However, the Lord chose to fulfill his promise to eventually birth the nation of Israel through Jacob. Jacob's twelve sons became the twelve tribes of Israel who would become a nation after entering the promised land.

The bold language of love and hatred in Malachi shows that God's plans formed long ago had been fulfilled as the Lord had promised. God loves all people, but his plan included a nation through the line of Jacob that continued to the nation of Israel. Through the seed of Abraham, the Messiah, Jesus Christ, came to earth and provided salvation for Jews and non-Jews (Romans 1:16).

God continues to bless the Jewish people, and many promises remain that he will one day fulfill. Today, we do not need to fear that the Lord hates us. We can experience his goodness in our lives when we believe in him by faith (Ephesians 2:8-9).

QUESTIONS ABOUT GOD

23. HOW DO WE KNOW THAT GOD EXISTS?

Atheistic skeptics continue to argue that there is no clear evidence to prove God's existence. Is this true?

Believers have used a variety of arguments to offer evidence for God's existence. However, the three most prominent claims include the argument from design, the causal argument, and the morality argument.

The argument from design is based on the view that every design has a designer. Since the universe reveals a highly complex design, someone or something must have designed it. This intelligent designer is God. From the farthest extents of the most powerful telescope's reach into space to the most powerful microscope's insights into the cell, the evidence points to intelligence rather than evolution. This argument does not prove the existence of the God of the Bible but does point toward an ultimate creative Being behind all things.

The causal argument claims that everything that exists has a cause. The universe exists. Therefore, the universe had a cause. The basic idea is that something does not come from nothing, resulting in the need for a first cause that Christians describe as God. The Bible describes

God as the first and the last, the beginning and the end. Genesis 1:1 says that God existed "in the beginning." Scripture clearly defines God as the first cause. Psalm 19 offers a biblical perspective of this argument. The first half of the psalm points to aspects of creation to affirm God's existence. For example, verse 1 reads, "The heavens declare the glory of God; and the firmament shows His handiwork." The second half of the psalm refers to God's word as being perfect.

A third argument is the morality argument. Every culture has inherent values of right and wrong, pointing to an absolute source of morality. This absolute lawgiver or source of absolute truth is God.

Though the Bible offers evidence for God through creation, miracles, Jesus, and other forms, Scripture often simply assumes his existence. For example, Genesis 1:1 begins by describing what God does without attempting to argue that he exists. In Psalm 14:1, the psalmist argued, "The fool has said in his heart, 'There is no God.'" In the New Testament, Hebrews 11:6 says, "Without faith it is impossible to please Him, for he who comes to God must believe that He is, and that He is a rewarder of those who diligently seek Him." Faith requires that we believe God is real.

Another way that the Bible describes the evidence for God is through the three c's—creation, conscience, and Christ. We know God exists because he is the best explanation for the creation of all things. Second, we can believe God is real because of the ultimate sense of morality found among all people. Third, Christ serves as the perfect evidence of God's existence and his love. Why? Because he came into our world to provide direct evidence of his life, actions, and power to defeat death and provide salvation.

24. DID GOD CREATE SIN?

If God is the creator of all things, does that mean he also created sin? Skeptics often ask this question, but so have sincere believers seeking to better understand the origin of sin in our world.

A look at the entry of sin into humanity helps to provide the best explanation. Eve was tempted by a serpent and, along with her husband, Adam, disobeyed the Lord's command. God did not tempt Eve; the serpent did. God created the serpent but not the temptation of the serpent, just as God created Adam and Eve but did not force them to sin.

But what about the serpent? How did it become involved with sin? The serpent is associated with Satan. Revelation 12:9 makes this explicitly clear: "The great dragon was cast out, that old serpent, called the Devil, and Satan, which deceiveth the whole world: he was cast out into the earth, and his angels were cast out with him" (KJV). Therefore, sin entered the world through Satan, but didn't God create Satan? Yes, God created Satan, but God did not originally create him to do evil. Though there is much unknown about Satan, God created him as Lucifer, "son of the morning," and he had the highest rank among the angels. In pride, he sought to rebel against God, becoming the originator of sin (Isaiah 14:12–17; Ezekiel 28:11–19).

James 1:13–14 also specifically teaches that God cannot be tempted by evil, nor does he tempt others: "Let no man say when he is tempted, I am tempted of God: for God cannot be tempted with evil, neither tempteth he any man: but every man is tempted, when he is drawn away of his own lust, and enticed" (KJV).

Sin entered humanity through Adam and Eve when they fell to Satan's temptation. All people now stand in need of salvation and the forgiveness of sin through faith in Jesus Christ. Romans 3:23 is clear that "all have sinned, and come short of the glory of God" (KJV). Romans 6:23 provides the consequences of sin and the answer to it: "For the wages of sin is death; but the gift of God is eternal life through Jesus Christ our Lord" (KJV).

It is also important to note that the entry of sin into our world did not take God by surprise. As the all-knowing Creator, he knew everything in advance. He has also provided the one and only answer to sin. Acts 4:12 teaches, "Nor is there salvation in any other, for there is no other name under heaven given among men by which we must be saved."

God offers salvation as a free gift of faith to all who will believe (Ephesians 2:8–9). When we believe, we receive new life (Romans 6:4; 2 Corinthians 5:17). God intends for us to share this new life with others, taking the message of God's love and redemption from sin to all nations (Matthew 28:19–20).

25. WHAT IS THE TRINITY?

Christians believe in the Trinity, but many do not understand what it is and where to read about it in the Bible. The Trinity is an important foundational tenet for believers and is key to better understanding God's nature and how we relate to him.

The Trinity refers to God the Father, God the Son, and God the Holy Spirit eternally existing equally as one God in three persons. Scripture does not specifically use the word *Trinity*, but the teaching is there in many parts of the Bible, and the New Testament especially reveals how Jesus and the Holy Spirit worked in the lives of Christians.

The Bible is clear that God the Father is the eternal God. From the first verse of Genesis, it is assumed that God is the ultimate Being who created the heavens and the earth. Jesus Christ is also referred to as God. John 1:1 says that "the Word was God," with "the Word" referring to

Jesus. Romans 9:5 refers to Jesus as "the eternally blessed God." The Holy Spirit is also God. In 1 Corinthians 3:16, the Spirit is called "the Spirit of God," whereas Acts 5:3–4 refers to the Spirit directly as God.

But if God the Father, Jesus, and the Holy Spirit are all three called "God," then how can they be one God? The Bible describes three persons but only one God (Deuteronomy 6:4; Galatians 3:20). There are not three gods but rather one God revealed in three persons.

Scripture refers to all three persons together in several New Testament passages. For example, Jesus ascended to heaven after telling his followers to baptize in the name of the Father, Son, and Holy Spirit (Matthew 28:19). Notice that Jesus said the "name," not the "names" of God, confirming there is one God in three persons.

In 1 Peter 1:2, the apostle mentioned that "the foreknowledge of God the Father, through sanctification of the Spirit, unto obedience and sprinkling of the blood of Jesus Christ" (KJV). All three persons of the triune Godhead are noted together as unique persons, though Peter clearly affirmed belief in one God.

On two occasions, the Father, Son, and Spirit all act in the same scene. The first occasion is at the baptism of Jesus. Jesus was baptized, the Spirit descended on him like a dove, and the voice of God the Father spoke from the sky (Matthew 3:16–17). The second occasion was at the transfiguration of Jesus. The voice of God spoke, Jesus was present, and the Spirit appeared in the form of a cloud (Luke 9:28–36).

Theologians and Bible teachers have used many illustrations to help explain the Trinity. For example, water can exist as a liquid, gas, or solid but remains water. However, there is no adequate comparison to explain the Trinity. The acknowledgment of one God in three persons, however, does emphasize community within the Godhead, illustrating the importance of our relationship with him and with other believers.

We know the Trinity exists because God has revealed the information in Scripture. We also experience God's Spirit in our lives as believers, observe God the Father's power in creation around us, and have testimony of God the Son coming to our world as a sacrifice for our sins.

26. WHAT DOES IT MEAN TO TEST GOD?

People sometimes talk about testing God, but what does this mean? Why does Scripture say we should not test the Lord?

In the Old Testament, Malachi 3:10 offers a clear example: "'Bring all the tithes into the storehouse, that there may be food in My house, and try Me now in this,' says the LORD of hosts, 'If I will not open for you the windows of heaven and pour out for you such blessing that there will not be room enough to receive it.'" In this situation, God condemned his people for not following his commands to give their tithe. He said if they would obey, he would bless them abundantly.

In the New Testament, Jesus spoke of testing when Satan tempted him in the wilderness. "Jesus answering said unto him, It is said, Thou shalt not tempt the Lord thy God" (Luke 4:12 KJV). Other translations use the word *test* instead of *tempt*. Jesus was quoting from Deuteronomy 6:16, which says, "You shall not tempt the LORD your God as you tempted Him in Massah."

Jesus knew that the law commanded the people not to treat God like the Jews had done at Massah. In Exodus 17:7, they asked, "Is the LORD among us or not?" Instead of trusting God to provide water, they challenged or dared him to provide, even questioning his ability, despite witnessing God literally move the waters of the Red Sea to rescue them.

How do these biblical teachings apply in our lives today? The example of Jesus and his temptation offers a clear example. When we face temptations or struggles in life, we are not to question God's plan or power. Instead, we are to trust in him, knowing he is all-powerful and mighty to save according to his will.

We test God when we question him and give him conditions, saying, "I'll do what you say if you do what I demand first." This is not how we are to respond to the Lord! He is God, and we are not. We don't demand that he do anything. Instead, we are to obey his teachings, as they are for our benefit, even when we don't always understand why things are happening in our lives.

We can also test God when we disobey him. God gave the prophet Jonah a clear command to preach to the people of Nineveh. Instead of obeying, Jonah ran away and experienced God's judgment. Jonah repented and was rescued, offering an example that was repeated when the people of Nineveh also repented and were spared from destruction.

Testing God reveals a lack of trust in God. Instead of questioning or debating God's commands, we experience his blessing in our lives when we obey. This may not mean an easy life; even Jesus suffered and died despite his obedience. However, we can know we are following God's will when we trust in him rather than doubting his power or goodness, leading to a fruitful life of service to the Lord and to others.

27. DOES GOD REALLY UNDERSTAND HOW I FEEL?

People often ask us if God really understands how we feel. We can certainly relate. Sometimes the Lord can seem distant, especially when we face big challenges in life. Thankfully, the Bible offers plenty of help to confirm God's love for us and understanding of our situation.

First, we know God can understand how we feel because he knows all things. For example, Acts 15:18 says, "Known to God from eternity are all His works." Romans 11:33 adds, "Oh, the depth of the riches both of the wisdom and knowledge of God! How unsearchable are His judgments and His ways past finding out!"

Second, we know God understands how we feel because Jesus came to experience our common humanity. John 1:14 says, "The Word became flesh and dwelt among us, and we beheld His glory, the glory as of the only begotten of the Father, full of grace and truth." The word translated "dwelt" is also the word used for "living among" or "setting up a tent." It could be rendered that "he pitched his tent among us." The Lord literally came to earth to live like we live, experiencing the emotions and concerns of human life.

Third, God knows how we feel because he created us. God is the creator of all things (Genesis 1:1). He has uniquely created you as well, sustaining you each moment of every day. He understands what excites you and what breaks your heart because he created your heart.

Fourth, God promises to work all things together for the good of those who love him. Romans 8:28 teaches, "We know that all things work together for good to those who love God, to those who are the called according to His purpose." We do not need to wonder whether God understands our feelings. We can trust that his plan takes into account every aspect of our being, including how we feel.

It is important to realize that God may understand how we feel, but he doesn't exist to simply make us feel happy. He is God, and we are not. We exist to please him.

At the same time, the Lord deeply cares about our emotions and well-being. He knows when we are sad and when we are hurt. Emotions are important, and God cares about them. In Scripture, God often used emotions to teach important lessons. For example, the prophet Jonah was upset that God relented and did not judge the people of Nineveh after he had preached to them. Surprisingly, the prophet said he was angry enough to die (Jonah 4:8). God then sent a plant to provide Jonah shade. The shade made him happy, but the plant soon died, and Jonah became angry again. God used the plant as an example of the importance of the people of Nineveh. Jonah was more upset over how his situation turned out than about the lives of over 120,000 people (Jonah 4:11).

We can find ourselves in a similar situation. When life is difficult, we tend to focus on why God is allowing us to go through a particular problem. Instead, we should remember that the Lord has his own purposes and that he intends to help us to serve him.

28. DOES ISAIAH 45:7 TEACH THAT GOD CREATED EVIL?

Isaiah 45:7 records God stating, "I form the light and create darkness, I make peace and create calamity; I, the LORD, do all these things." Does this mean God created evil?

There are two parts to answering this question. First, does Isaiah 45:7 address the creation of evil? This is unlikely. The contrast between peace and calamity appears to focus on God controlling times of war and peace among the Jewish people. Isaiah often addresses this concern, especially as the nation of Israel lived under the threat of the king of Babylon.

Second, even if this verse is not directly discussing the origin of evil, does God create evil? There is a distinction in Scripture between God making all things and God making evil. While the Lord is clearly the creator of the heavens and the earth and everything in them, he did not directly create evil.

Where did evil originate? Jesus called Satan the father of lies in John 8:44: "You are of your father the devil, and the desires of your father you want to do. He was a murderer from the beginning, and does not stand in the truth, because there is no truth in him. When he speaks a lie, he speaks from his own resources, for he is a liar and the father of it." Jesus is clear that Satan is the one who is behind evil in our world. Yes, God created Satan, but Satan is the one who originated sin among humanity.

We find the account of Satan introducing sin into our world in Genesis 3. He was the serpent who tempted Adam and Eve in the garden of Eden, which allowed sin to begin among people. God judged the serpent in the garden, and Satan will experience a final judgment at the end of time. Did you know that Satan will one day be cast into an eternal lake of fire? Revelation 20:10 predicts, "The devil that deceived them was cast into the lake of fire and brimstone, where the beast and the false prophet are, and shall be tormented day and night for ever and ever" (KJV).

Satan is the tempter and deceiver, whereas Jesus is the one who cannot fall to temptation. This contrast is seen in the temptation of Jesus in the wilderness (Matthew 4:1–10). Jesus was tempted by Satan and resisted him. James 1:13 adds, "God cannot be tempted by evil, nor does He Himself tempt anyone."

God did not create evil, nor does he tolerate it. He has a plan that will one day remove all evil and will break the curse of sin. Until then, we live in a good but fallen world in which God calls every person to faith in Jesus Christ to receive freedom from the curse of sin and experience both new life in this world and eternal life with the Lord after this world.

29. DOES GOD TEMPT US TO SIN? WHAT ABOUT ABRAHAM IN GENESIS 22?

Many people claim that God doesn't tempt people to sin, but what about the account of Abraham in Genesis 22? God told Abraham to sacrifice his own son Isaac as a burnt offering. Wasn't this wrong?

Bible scholars have answered this question in a variety of ways. The Ten Commandments clearly state, "You shall not murder" (Exodus 20:13). Some suggest that God was not telling Abraham to sin, however, because the Ten Commandments were not written until much later. This option appears to be an inadequate response. When Cain killed his brother Abel, God condemned Cain. Lamech also expressed his guilt after murdering someone (Genesis 4:23–24). Genesis 6 confirms that there was plenty of evidence that murder was a sin long before the Ten Commandments.

A more accurate explanation is found in Hebrews 11:17–19: "By faith Abraham, when he was tested, offered up Isaac, and he who had received the promises offered up his only begotten son, of whom it was said, 'In Isaac your seed shall be called,' concluding that God was able to raise him up, even from the dead, from which he also received him in a figurative sense." The author of Hebrews made a clear distinction between Abraham being tested and Abraham being tempted.

James 1:13 directly teaches that God does not tempt people to sin. Instead, God tested Abraham by asking him to give up his only son. Abraham had become a father in a miraculous way, with his wife being ninety years old when she gave birth to Isaac. To consider losing his son was the worst tragedy Abraham could face. When God called Abraham to give up Isaac, however, Scripture tells us that he "rose early in the morning" (Genesis 22:3). He clearly heard from God and directly obeyed.

The end of the account clearly reveals that God never intended for Abraham to kill his own son. Why not? First, God stopped Abraham before he could go through with the sacrifice. Second, God had already placed a ram nearby for Abraham to use as an offering instead of Isaac (Genesis 22:13).

God's blessing upon Abraham for his obedience was powerful: "By Myself I have sworn, says the LORD, because you have done this thing, and have not withheld your son, your only son—blessing I will bless you, and multiplying I will multiply your descendants as the stars of the heaven and as the sand which is on the seashore; and your descendants shall possess the gate of their enemies. In your seed all the nations of the earth shall be blessed, because you have obeyed My voice" (Genesis 22:16–18).

God not only blessed Abraham for his faithfulness. He also promised to bless him with countless descendants and to bless the entire world through him. Even the Messiah Jesus would come from the family line of Abraham, literally fulfilling the promise that his descendants would bless "all the nations."

30. WHY DOES GOD ALLOW PEOPLE TO SUFFER?

We all struggle at times with the concept of God allowing people to suffer. We read in Scripture that God is good and controls all things, but the events in our lives don't always feel like God is looking out for us. Why does God allow us to suffer?

Suffering is not enjoyable but does serve as part of God's plan. We see a clear example of this in the account of Noah and the ark. God saved Noah and his family despite bringing judgment on all the earth. They certainly did not enjoy suffering for many months inside the ark, but they were saved and became examples of God's mercy during times of judgment.

The life of Joseph is another biblical example. His own brothers sold him as a slave. He was later falsely accused of sexual assault and sent to prison. Even those he helped in prison forgot about him. Yet at the right time, one of the men he interpreted a dream for and helped in prison remembered Joseph when Pharaoh needed a dream interpreter.

How did God answer in the life of Joseph? Despite thirteen years of slavery and imprisonment, Joseph became second in charge of the entire nation of Egypt in a single day. He was eventually reunited with his family, saved the nation of Egypt, and served as the person who rescued his own family during the famine. His actions ultimately led to the expansion of the Jewish people in Egypt until they grew large enough to become their own nation.

The apostle Paul also noted that the suffering he faced would not compare with the glory that awaits believers in eternity. "For I consider that the sufferings of this present time are not worthy to be compared with the glory which shall be revealed in us" (Romans 8:18). Paul taught in 2 Corinthians 1:3–4 that the suffering we face allows us to better help others who have suffered in similar ways: "Blessed be the God and Father of our Lord Jesus Christ, the Father of mercies and God of all comfort, who comforts us in all our tribulation, that we may be able to comfort those who are in any trouble, with the comfort with which we ourselves are comforted by God."

For example, a cancer survivor can better encourage another person going through cancer. The mother who has lost a child to early death can better relate to someone facing a similar loss. These kinds of suffering are not enjoyable, but they do allow us to uniquely serve others facing similar pains.

Jesus served as the ultimate example of suffering, fulfilling a crucial role in the Lord's will for humanity. He suffered the most brutal end of all, which included being beaten and whipped, having to wear a crown of thorns, having nails driven through his feet and hands, and hanging on a cross. Despite his intense suffering, his pain led not only to his death but also to his resurrection. The resurrection of Jesus proved once and for all that he is God's Son. We are called sometimes to suffer as well, knowing that God works through both good and bad circumstances to fulfill his perfect plan.

It is also important to remember that the suffering we face will one day end. Revelation 21:3–4 promises, "Behold, the tabernacle of God is with men, and he will dwell with them, and they shall be his people, and God himself shall be with them, and be their God. And God shall wipe away all tears from their eyes; and there shall be no more death, neither sorrow, nor crying, neither shall there be any more pain: for the former things are passed away" (KJV).

31.   WHY DID GOD ALLOW SLAVERY IN BIBLICAL TIMES?

We want to be very clear that the Bible does not teach that people should own slaves. Slavery is discussed in Scripture, but Scripture does not teach that slavery is something a person following God should practice.

The Old Testament often mentions servants or slaves. The Jewish people were forced into harsh slavery under Pharaoh in Egypt, with God rescuing them through Moses. When Moses wrote the law for the Israelites, he gave clear commands for the Israelites not to mistreat any servants or slaves they may have.

The Jewish people entered the promised land under Joshua and defeated their opponents in war. These successes in war often resulted in the Israelites enslaving defeated opponents instead of completely destroying them. In addition, in Joshua 9, the Gibeonites voluntarily became servants of Israel to avoid destruction.

Some people also became slaves through debt bondage. These servants could work off their debt, and the practice was intended as short-term rather than lifelong under normal circumstances. Under the Mosaic law, anyone owning a Jewish servant had to set the servant free in the seventh year (Exodus 21:2). Slaves also had to be set free in the year of Jubilee (Leviticus 25:39–41).

In the New Testament, the apostle Paul condemned those who bought and sold people. In 1 Timothy, Paul said, "We also know that the law is made not for the righteous but for lawbreakers and...for slave traders and liars and perjurers—and for whatever else is contrary to the sound doctrine" (vv. 1:9-10 NIV). In the letter to Philemon, the New Testament's shortest book, Paul provided his strongest words against slavery in a society where bondage was common. In this book, a slave named Onesimus ran away from his Christian owner Philemon. During his journey, Onesimus met Paul and became a follower of Jesus. Paul wrote to the Christian slave owner, saying in verses 8-11, "Therefore, though I might be very bold in Christ to command you what is fitting, yet for love's sake I rather appeal to you—being such a one as Paul, the aged, and now also a prisoner of Jesus Christ—I appeal to you for my son Onesimus, whom I have begotten while in my chains, who once was unprofitable to you, but now is profitable to you and to me."

Notice several aspects of Paul's letter. First, he referred to what was "fitting." Paul implied that the right thing was to free Onesimus from slavery and the punishment he could face for fleeing from his owner.

Second, Paul appealed to Philemon based on love. In other words, he did not have the legal right to force Philemon to free Onesimus. Instead, he asked him "for love's sake" to voluntarily do it.

Third, Paul viewed the slave Onesimus as "profitable" for both of them but not as a slave. Paul referred to the man as a fellow brother in the Lord. Verse 16 adds that Paul saw Onesimus as "no longer as a slave but more than a slave—a beloved brother, especially to me but how much more to you, both in the flesh and in the Lord."

Fourth, verse 17 says that Paul wanted Onesimus to view himself as an equal to Paul: "If then you count me as a partner, receive him as you would me." In a culture that allowed slavery, Paul identified a slave as his equal and advocated for his freedom.

Unlike those living in free societies today who can advocate for changed laws, Paul and other early Christians instead had to work within their culture's legal system to advocate for the freedom of slaves whenever possible and for the humane treatment of those who remained in slavery. It should be no surprise that Christians have been key in helping to eliminate slavery in almost every culture where the practice has been abolished.

From William Wilberforce in England to the Christian abolitionists of America's history, people of faith have been an essential part of freeing slaves. Still today, many believers are involved in the fight against human trafficking in efforts to end modern-day slavery as an important part of living out the teachings of God's Word.

32. WHY DOES GOD PERMIT NATURAL DISASTERS LIKE HURRICANES, EARTHQUAKES, AND TSUNAMIS?

God made all things and can control all things. Why does he allow natural disasters that harm and kill people, harm animals, and destroy homes and nature?

There are several ways to address this question, but we must begin by acknowledging that there are often no answers that are agreeable when we face tragedies related to natural disasters. We have personally ministered to many people who have endured hardship and loss due to tornadoes and hurricanes and realize these are times of grief and other high emotions. However, even in these dark situations, God is with us.

God sometimes allowed natural disasters in Scripture for several reasons. A natural disaster might be due to God's judgment. For example, the flood during Noah's time was a judgment upon sin, with God saving only a few people. God also once used an earthquake as judgment against those who had sinned against him (Numbers 16:30–34).

God also used natural disasters in Scripture so people would hear his voice. When Elijah stood before the Lord in 1 Kings 19:11–12, God sent a wind, an earthquake, and a fire before speaking to Elijah in a still, small voice. When God spoke, it empowered the prophet to continue his ministry, returning to his land with renewed strength.

These might also be valid reasons why God would allow tragedies of nature in our modern time, but there are other explanations as well. For one, natural disasters are simply part of the actions of our natural world. Even wildfires, which often lead to losses of homes or lives, are part of nature's process of renewal in many parts of the world. The actions themselves are neither good nor bad. Instead, we are generally concerned only when natural disasters affect our lives or the lives of others we know.

God may also allow natural disasters to open opportunities for Christians to show godly compassion. Christians are often at the forefront of disaster relief. Why? It's an opportunity to share God's love with hurting people. It's also an expression of Matthew 25:37–40, where Jesus calls us to show Christ's love to all. The practice is even an expression of loving our neighbor as ourselves.

A final reason why God allows natural disasters is to cause people to turn to him for help. In Mark 4:35–41, the disciples were crossing a sea in a boat with Jesus. A great storm came upon the water and threatened to sink their boat. They woke up Jesus, who was sleeping in the boat, turning to him for help. How did Jesus respond? In their case, he spoke and stopped the storm. The action led the disciples to recognize Christ's power over the wind and the sea as part of his power as God in human form. God sent the storm to increase their faith, not to destroy them. God can send storms as part of his natural processes in the world, for judgment or even for good in our lives, if we are willing to listen to his voice.

We may face some storms or natural disasters in life to point us closer to our heavenly Father. We've seen many people turn to the Lord following a natural disaster, with God using the tragic event to change hearts for eternity. While we do not desire such disasters, God has a perfect plan that is at work even during these difficult events.

SECTION 5

QUESTIONS ABOUT
THE HOLY SPIRIT

33. WILL WE BE ABLE TO SEE THE HOLY SPIRIT IN HEAVEN?

Jesus now sits in heaven at the right hand of his Father, where believers will one day be in his presence, but what about the Holy Spirit? Will we be able to see the Spirit in heaven in the same way?

The Holy Spirit does not have a body like Jesus, but that does not mean he is invisible. For example, the Spirit sometimes revealed himself in visible forms in Scripture. In Genesis 1:2, we read, "The Spirit of God was hovering over the face of the waters." The verse doesn't specifically say the Spirit was visible, but he may have had some form because he was hovering. During the exodus, the presence or Spirit of God was visible over the Jewish people daily. He existed in the form of a cloud, offering a constant reminder of the Lord's presence, as well as guidance from place to place during their wilderness journey.

During the life of Jesus, two interesting accounts are mentioned about the Holy Spirit. When Jesus was baptized, the Spirit came down upon Jesus in the form of a dove (Matthew 3:16). It is uncertain whether the New

Testament gospel writers meant the Spirit looked like a bird or whether the Spirit came down visibly as a form of light. In either case, the Spirit appeared in a visible form. During the transfiguration, Matthew 17:5 states, "While he was still speaking, behold, a bright cloud overshadowed them; and suddenly a voice came out of the cloud, saying, 'This is My beloved Son, in whom I am well pleased. Hear Him!'" God the Father, God the Spirit, and God the Son were all three present, with the Spirit appearing in the form of a cloud.

Revelation 21:23 mentions that "the glory of God" will illuminate the future New Jerusalem, where all God's people will ultimately dwell with him for eternity. This may be a reference to the Spirit, as God the Father and the Lamb (Jesus) are mentioned in the previous verse.

Based on what we have seen throughout Scripture, it is likely that the Holy Spirit will reveal himself in some form in heaven but probably not in a bodily form like Jesus. Perhaps the Spirit will appear in a cloudlike form similar to the way God's Spirit traveled with the Jewish people in the wilderness.

It is also important to remember that all believers will have new bodies in heaven. These new spiritual bodies may also be able to see and experience God in ways that we are unable to perceive in our current earthly bodies.

The evidence from Scripture points toward the Holy Spirit being with us in a clear form in heaven. However, the Spirit will not be in the form of a human being but will appear in an unspecified way that will be evident to those who dwell with the Lord for all eternity.

34. WILL THE HOLY SPIRIT STILL BE AT WORK ON THE EARTH DURING THE TRIBULATION?

Some have questioned whether the Spirit will continue to operate in our world during the future tribulation because of 2 Thessalonians 2:7. Does this verse teach that the Holy Spirit will stop working during this time?

The verse reads, "The mystery of lawlessness is already at work; only He who now restrains will do so until He is taken out of the way." Most interpreters agree that the restrainer in this verse refers to the Holy Spirit. The context of the surrounding verses speaks of the tribulation, so some have concluded that the Spirit will no longer be present in our world during this future time. But that's not exactly what the verse says. It emphasizes that "He who now restrains" (the Holy Spirit) will at some point be "taken out of the way." The Spirit will not leave our world but will stop holding back the lawless one, the Antichrist, from unleashing evil.

There are also other reasons we can know that the Spirit will not stop working on the earth during the tribulation. For example, the Holy Spirit is the third person of the one triune God consisting of the Father, Son, and Spirit. God, including the Spirit, is omnipresent, meaning always present. The Spirit may stop working in a certain way at a particular time but will never leave us.

In addition, the Bible is clear that the Holy Spirit will still be at work during the tribulation. This seven-year period will include much judgment, but God will save many people. This will include 144,000 Jewish males who will serve as leaders of revival during the tribulation. Revelation 7:4 says, "I heard the number of those who were sealed. One hundred and forty-four thousand of all the tribes of the children of Israel were sealed."

In addition, many people from all nations will come to faith in the Lord during the future tribulation. Verses

9–10 say, "After these things I looked, and behold, a great multitude which no one could number, of all nations, tribes, peoples, and tongues, standing before the throne and before the Lamb, clothed with white robes, with palm branches in their hands, and crying out with a loud voice, saying, 'Salvation belongs to our God who sits on the throne, and to the Lamb!'"

The Holy Spirit definitely works in the life of every person who experiences salvation. The miracle of conversion includes conviction (feeling bad about your sin and then desiring reconciliation with God); repentance (turning from sin to faith in Christ); and, when we put our faith in Jesus, regeneration (this means that our soul changes from a state of death to that state of being alive). God's Holy Spirit indwells and seals the believer. In fact, all the aforementioned works that take place within a person who turns to the Lord are actions carried out by the Holy Spirit.

Since all these components of salvation will be taking place in the lives of some people during the tribulation, it is clear that God's Holy Spirit will be present and ministering on planet earth.

God's Spirit will also work in other ways during the tribulation. For example, the two witnesses in Revelation 11 will operate by God's Spirit to display miracles. They will even be able to stop rain from falling, similar to Elijah's prediction of no rain in the Old Testament. Verse 3 teaches, "I will give power to my two witnesses, and they will prophesy one thousand two hundred and sixty days, clothed in sackcloth." Their ministry will extend through the first three and a half years of the tribulation before their death, resurrection, and ascension to heaven (vv. 11–12).

The Holy Spirit will work in a different way during the future tribulation, but he will not leave. God's Spirit will be ever present, indwelling believers and operating to fulfill God's plan even during the difficult days of the tribulation.

35. CAN A CHRISTIAN LOSE THE HOLY SPIRIT?

Many people have asked us if a Christian can lose the Holy Spirit. The concern usually comes from reading Psalm 51:11, where David said to God, "Do not cast me away from Your presence, and do not take Your Holy Spirit from me." If David was concerned about losing God's Spirit, should we be worried about this too?

This important question includes several key areas of biblical teaching. It is important to first understand that the Holy Spirit worked differently before coming to indwell believers in the New Testament. In David's time, God's Spirit sometimes specially empowered a person for a particular time or task. As king, David had received God's special capability to lead Israel. After his sin involving Bathsheba, he repented. Asking God for forgiveness, David pleaded with the Lord not to take this special presence of his Spirit away. David had previously witnessed God removing this special blessing of his Spirit from King Saul: "The Spirit of the Lord departed from Saul, and an evil spirit from the Lord troubled him" (1 Samuel 16:14 KJV). Saul had disobeyed God and was no longer led by the Spirit in the same way as he had been previously.

A similar situation happened in the life of Samson. God gave Samson special power and strength through the Spirit to defeat Israel's enemies. After Delilah cut off his hair, this empowerment of the Holy Spirit left him. "So he awoke from his sleep, and said, 'I will go out as before, at other times, and shake myself free!' But he did not know that the Lord had departed from him" (Judges 16:20).

In the New Testament, the Holy Spirit gave birth to the church on the day of Pentecost in Acts 2. Jesus had told the disciples that the Father would send the Holy Spirit to be with them forever (John 14:16). The apostle Paul later wrote, "In Him you also trusted, after you heard the word of truth, the gospel of your salvation; in whom also, having believed, you were sealed with the Holy Spirit of promise, who is the guarantee of our inheritance until the redemption of the purchased possession, to the praise of His glory" (Ephesians 1:13–14). The Holy Spirit does not leave believers.

Ephesians 4:30 later adds, "Do not grieve the Holy Spirit of God, by whom you were sealed for the day of redemption." We can sadden God's Spirit within us as believers, but we can never lose him.

This is also why we hold the view that a true believer in the Lord never loses his or her salvation. We may stumble, but God's Spirit continues to work within us to help us in our weakness. Though there are some who claim to be followers of Christ who later turn away, proving they were never believers, God never casts away his children and never takes back his gift of salvation, including the indwelling of his Spirit within us.

36. What Is the Fruit of the Holy Spirit?

The fruit (not fruits) of the Spirit is found in Galatians 5:22–23: "The fruit of the Spirit is love, joy, peace, longsuffering, kindness, goodness, faithfulness, gentleness, self-control. Against such there is no law." What do these traits mean for our lives today?

The same Greek word translated "fruit" can also be understood as "result." These nine traits are what others will see in us when God's Spirit controls our lives. Every Christian has God's Spirit living within them (Romans 8:9–10). Therefore, every believer should grow in these traits.

These positive areas also contrast with sinful actions in the preceding verses of Galatians 5. Verses 19–21 teach, "Now the works of the flesh are evident, which are: adultery, fornication, uncleanness, lewdness, idolatry, sorcery, hatred, contentions, jealousies, outbursts of wrath, selfish ambitions, dissensions, heresies, envy, murders, drunkenness, revelries, and the like; of which I tell you beforehand, just as I also told you in time past, that those who practice such things will not inherit the kingdom of God."

Notice what Paul said about these negative, sinful practices. First, he taught they are "evident." Sinful habits are usually obvious. Paul listed several to give examples, but he did not intend for his list to cover every possible wrong a person could commit. Second, these negative practices were not to be known among God's people. In fact, Paul clearly added that those known for such sinful lifestyles were not believers and would not be in heaven with the Lord. As believers, we still sin, but we also fight against sinful practices and seek to do what is right, living in the power of God's Spirit. Others should not know us for our sinful practices.

Even in the Old Testament, the woman known as Rahab the prostitute believed in the Lord of Israel and was saved from the destruction of the city of Jericho. No matter our past, God can change us when we believe in Jesus Christ (John 3:16). When we do, we begin to desire to do what is right, choosing to live more like the traits found in the fruit of the Spirit.

In Romans 7:14–25, the apostle Paul provided a good description of what it is like as followers of Jesus in our battle against sinful temptations. He said that he found himself still sinning even when he was trying to do what was right, proving that sin continues even after we choose to believe in Christ and live for the Lord. Verses 19–20 state, "For the good that I will to do, I do not do; but the evil I will not to do, that I practice. Now if I do what I will not to do, it is no longer I who do it, but sin that dwells in me." These words might sound confusing, but they are often true in our daily lives. We want to live out the traits of the fruit of the Spirit as believers, yet we continue to face the temptations of our world. By relying on God's Spirit, spending time with

God's people, and studying God's truth, we increasingly seek to show the fruit of the Spirit in our lives in ways that honor our heavenly Father and point other people to him: "Let your light so shine before men, that they may see your good works, and glorify your Father which is in heaven" (Matthew 5:16 KJV).

37. WHAT DOES IT MEAN TO BE FILLED WITH THE SPIRIT?

One important aspect of Christian living is the concept of being filled with the Spirit. The apostle Paul mentioned it in Ephesians 5:18, but what does it mean for our lives?

The verse reads, "Do not be drunk with wine, in which is dissipation; but be filled with the Spirit." Paul contrasted drinking too much, or being drunk, with being filled with the Spirit. We are not to be controlled by alcohol but rather by the Lord. This emphasis on control is key. When we focus on God's Spirit being in charge of our lives, we can more clearly understand God's plans for our lives and obey him accordingly.

Is there a way to be filled with the Spirit? First, it's important to note that every believer already has the Spirit living within them. Jesus promised in John 14:16, "I will pray the Father, and He will give you another Helper, that He may abide with you forever." Once we receive the Spirit, we don't lose him. We are either obedient and controlled by the Spirit, or we disobey God and are controlled by other areas of life.

Paul did not give an exact formula for how to be filled with the Spirit. Instead, he offered several areas of focus in Ephesian 5. Verses 19–21 emphasize speaking and singing spiritual songs, giving thanks to God, and submitting to one another. The remainder of the chapter focuses on a proper relationship between a Christian husband and wife. The following chapter, Ephesians 6, focuses on teachings for children, parents, servants, and masters and concludes with an emphasis on the spiritual armor of God (vv. 10–20).

It appears that the important factors for being filled with the Spirit include worshiping with other believers, cultivating godly family and work relationships, and maintaining a personal focus on prayer and God's Word as part of God's spiritual armor. There is no single secret to special access to the Holy Spirit, regardless of what some spiritual teachers may claim. Living according to God's Spirit involves the daily battle of choosing what is right and obeying the Lord and his teachings in the face of intense spiritual conflict.

On a related note, however, it is also helpful to point out that many people in Scripture found spiritual renewal through special time alone with God. For example, Moses had a special tent of meeting where he prayed to the Lord (Exodus 33:7–11). Elijah heard the Lord's voice after a long journey alone with the Lord. Luke 5:16 says that Jesus "often withdrew into the wilderness and prayed."

While we are made for community and relationships that can help us grow spiritually, we also sometimes need time away from others to recharge and refocus on the Lord. When we are alone with the Lord, we are never truly alone. We instead remove the noise of other voices to focus on God's voice in a fresh way. This practice can help us to better allow the Spirit to control us or fill us as we pray, meditate on God's Word, and humble ourselves before him.

We are to be filled with the Spirit as believers, a practice that takes diligent effort, intense focus, and frequent reminders in order to remain faithful and fruitful in our walk with the Lord and our service to others.

38. HOW CAN A PERSON WALK IN THE SPIRIT?

Galatians 5:25–26 tells Christians to walk in the Spirit, saying, "If we live in the Spirit, let us also walk in the Spirit. Let us not become conceited, provoking one another, envying one another." What does it mean to walk in the Spirit?

The apostle Paul focused on both living and walking. To live in the Spirit means we daily seek to obey God's plans for our lives. To walk in the Spirit includes the practical steps necessary to stay on the spiritual path. Ephesians uses the word *walk* eight times to emphasize the ongoing aspects of holy living.

In Ephesians 2:2 Paul said the believers reading his letter "once walked according to the course of this world." In other words, they followed the sinful ways of their society rather than God's teachings.

Verse 10 adds, "We are His workmanship, created in Christ Jesus for good works, which God prepared beforehand that we should walk in them." God has prepared good works for us to "walk in," or perform. Amazingly, he prepared these works for us before the foundations of the world.

Ephesians 4:1 calls believers "to walk worthy of the calling with which you were called." In contrast with unfaithful living, believers are to stay on God's path and follow the truth of his Word.

Verse 17 then uses the word *walk* twice: "This I say, therefore, and testify in the Lord, that you should no longer walk as the rest of the Gentiles walk, in the futility of their mind." Again, Paul contrasted walking like unbelievers with the worthy walk required of Christ's followers.

Ephesians 5:2 calls believers to "walk in love, as Christ also has loved us and given Himself for us." This high calling to follow the example of Jesus and his ultimate sacrifice on the cross reminds us that our spiritual walk is not easy but includes many difficulties.

Verse 8 then calls us to "walk as children of light."

Verse 15 adds that we should "walk circumspectly," meaning to move forward with wisdom.

All eight occurrences emphasize the need to avoid following sinful temptations and to persistently remain on God's path. The concept of walking was well-known to Paul and other travelers of his day. Without cars or planes, Paul walked thousands of miles during his missionary journeys to bring the gospel to new people and help them in their walk with the Lord. In a society in which walking was a daily necessity and a major part of life, Paul turned the practice into an illustration of the ongoing importance of not walking in sin but rather walking along God's path for our lives in faithful obedience to God's Spirit.

39. WHAT DOES IT MEAN TO QUENCH THE SPIRIT?

In 1 Thessalonians 5:19 the apostle Paul spoke of quenching the Holy Spirit: "Do not quench the Spirit." What did he mean, and how does this apply to our lives today as followers of Christ?

First, clearly, quenching God's Spirit is a negative thing. In verses 19–22, Paul noted three additional concerns that include not despising prophecies, testing all things to hold to what is good, and abstaining from evil.

Second, we can't stop God from working, but we often negatively affect our own lives through disobedience that stops his Spirit from more fully working in us. This disobedience can also harm the lives of those around us. The Greek word translated "quench" refers to putting out a fire (Matthew 12:20; Hebrews 11:34). Isaiah 43:17 speaks of a candle being "quenched like a wick." When the oxygen is removed from the flame, the fire goes out. In a similar way, when we sin, our disobedience produces a situation in which God does not work in us in the same way as when we obediently serve him.

Third, the concept of quenching the Spirit may echo teachings from the Old Testament. When the Israelites complained in Numbers 11, fire consumed some of the people. In verse 2, Scripture tells us, "The people cried out to Moses, and when Moses prayed to the Lord, the fire was quenched." In Jeremiah, God spoke of his judgment on the temple and the Jewish people for their ongoing disobedience. God warned, "Lest my fury go out like fire, and burn that none can quench it, because of the evil of your doings" (Jeremiah 21:12 KJV).

In a similar way, Paul's warning in 1 Thessalonians 5:19 is that we should not live in disobedience to the Lord if we wish to avoid God's judgment and experience his power at work in our lives. When we faithfully follow his truth and teachings, God's Spirit remains alive and burns with passion through us to impact many others. Even though we may "quiet" the Spirit, the Spirit, nevertheless, is always present in the life of a believer.

James 1:22 warns, "Be doers of the word, and not hearers only, deceiving yourselves." We are saved by grace alone through faith alone in Christ alone: "For by grace you have been saved through faith, and that not of yourselves; it is the gift of God, not of works, lest anyone should boast" (Ephesians 2:8–9). However, our faithful obedience keeps God's Spirit at work through us like a powerful flame that those around us can clearly see through our lives.

In John 12:46 Jesus taught, "I have come as a light into the world, that whoever believes in Me should not abide in darkness." When we follow the Lord, he is a light within us, burning bright. Let us not quench this fire within us, but let us walk humbly before him to fulfill his calling for our lives.

40. WHAT ARE THE GIFTS OF THE SPIRIT?

The New Testament provides various lists that include spiritual gifts God gives to believers to use in serving others. While the lists may not be exhaustive, they offer examples of the types of abilities God gives his followers to live out his will and reach others for the Lord.

The first passage that mentions spiritual gifts is Romans 12:6–8: "Having then gifts differing according to the grace that is given to us, let us use them: if prophecy, let us prophesy in proportion to our faith; or ministry, let us use it in our ministering; he who teaches, in teaching; he who exhorts, in exhortation; he who gives, with liberality; he who leads, with diligence; he who shows mercy, with cheerfulness." Paul clearly noted that the gifts of prophecy, ministry, teaching, exhorting (or encouraging), giving, leadership, and mercy are seven spiritual gifts.

A second passage that lists spiritual gifts is 1 Corinthians 12:4–11. Paul mentioned wisdom, knowledge, faith, healings, miracles, prophecy, discerning of spirits, tongues (or languages), and the interpretation of tongues. These nine gifts duplicate some of the gifts in his previous passage while mentioning additional gifts used in the church.

A third passage that some include among those discussing gifts of the Spirit is Ephesians 4:11–12: "He Himself gave some to be apostles, some prophets, some evangelists, and some pastors and teachers, for the equipping of the saints for the work of ministry." While the passage discusses gifts, the areas of apostles, prophets, evangelists, and pastor-teachers appear to focus on leadership roles that may include a variety of gifts.

A fourth passage that addresses spiritual gifts is provided by the apostle Peter in 1 Peter 4:10–11: "As each one has received a gift, minister it to one another, as good stewards of the manifold grace of God. If anyone speaks, let him speak as the oracles of God. If anyone ministers, let him do it as with the ability which God supplies, that in all things God may be glorified through Jesus Christ, to whom belong the glory and the dominion forever and ever. Amen." He mentioned speaking and ministering (or serving) as two important gifts within the church. Some see these two gifts as repeating the gifts of teaching and serving mentioned elsewhere by Paul.

A study of these areas allows us to make some important observations about spiritual gifts. First, every believer has at least one gift. Second, the variety of gifts in the lists seems to indicate these are examples of many ways God may gift people to serve. For example, music is not listed, but many are gifted in this area for service to the Lord. Third, the purpose of gifts is to honor God and serve others, not to reach self-serving goals. We like to say that we are blessed to be a blessing. Many people debate whether certain gifts are still in use today. While this is an important consideration, the emphasis in Scripture is on using our abilities as faithful stewards of God's blessing upon our lives.

The Lord has given you unique abilities to influence lives for eternity. You don't need to worry about a test to figure out how God has gifted you. Simply serve based on what you can do best and let him take care of the rest. God wants to work through you as part of the ultimate team of believers who bring people to know the true and living God who provides all gifts: "Every good gift and every perfect gift is from above, and comes down from the Father of lights, with whom there is no variation or shadow of turning" (James 1:17).

41.   Does every Christian have a spiritual gift?

The Bible discusses much about spiritual gifts, but does every believer have a spiritual gift? How can we know?

We love how 1 Peter 4:10 responds to this question: "As each one has received a gift, minister it to one another, as good stewards of the manifold grace of God." Peter clearly believed that every believer has a gift and is called to use their gift or gifts to live for the Lord. There is no doubt in God's Word that you have a gift if you are a believer. Even unbelievers have amazing talents and abilities. Those who follow the Lord also have God's Spirit living within them to provide supernatural power to affect lives.

Those who doubt whether they have a spiritual gift usually struggle with one of two issues. First, a person who doubts their spiritual gifts may be dealing with discouragement. It's easy to see God at work in the lives of others, but we often miss how he is operating in our own lives. Even worse, we can compare ourselves with others and miss out on the unique ways the Lord is calling us to serve.

A second reason people struggle with whether every believer has a spiritual gift is when they don't know what gift or gifts they have. New or young believers especially face doubts regarding what they can do well. We like to encourage people to serve where they are and watch how God blesses their efforts. For example, it doesn't take a special degree to help hand out bulletins at church or to help set up chairs for an event. We can all serve to help our brothers and sisters in Christ with practical needs as well, whether in sharing food with the hungry or shoveling snow from a person's driveway. Through our everyday acts of kindness, God often reveals how we are gifted to serve best.

I (Alex) came to faith in the Lord during college. At first, I didn't know how to best serve God, but through helping out in my church and in different college activities, I discovered the Lord would distinctly use me through speaking opportunities. Years later, I sensed God calling me to attempt a major step of faith—sharing the gospel by preaching in fifty states in fifty days. I did, and this journey became the launching point for decades of serving God through communication by public speaking, radio, television, writing, and online.[4]

God may also use the encouragement of others to help you recognize your giftedness. As others notice that we are great at art or construction or working with children or leading a business, they may affirm the ways the Lord wants us to serve. This is another reason it is important to be involved in a local church with other believers who can help you discover and grow in your spiritual gifts.

It's not about where you begin. It's where you end. Start serving where you are by using your natural abilities and allow God to show you how you are most effective in his plan to impact eternity.

---

4 Alex McFarland and Bert Harper can be heard live Monday through Friday on radio stations throughout North America. Archived shows are available on www.afr.net, and you can access much video and audio content by the authors on all popular digital platforms.

SECTION 6

QUESTIONS ABOUT WORLDVIEW

42. HOW DO I RESPOND TO SOMEONE WHO SAYS, "IT'S TRUE FOR YOU BUT NOT FOR ME. I HAVE MY OWN TRUTH"?

We live in a culture where more people are suggesting that something can be true for you but not for them. People talk about speaking "their truth," but this is far different from how Scripture defines truth. How can we respond to this trend?

It's important to define *truth*. Many people give different descriptions, but truth is simply something that is in accordance with reality. In other words, two plus two equals four, unless we are ready to start redefining math! But truth goes far beyond the observable facts of math or agreeing on which day of the week it is. Unless we have a shared foundation for evaluating truth, we simply won't agree. If we find ourselves at the impasse of "your truth" versus "my truth," mutual acknowledgment of "God's truth" is the best way to resolve the dilemma.

This is why believers look to Scripture to define truth. John 14:6 says Jesus is the way and the truth and the life. He is not merely a way; he is the Way. How does commitment to

Jesus inform one's beliefs about moral issues? It relates to the nature of God, moral truth, and the revelation of Scripture.

God's nature is righteous and holy, and the Bible says that in God "is no darkness at all" (1 John 1:5). Actions that are truly moral and "right" are those that are in conformity with the holy character of God. Since we learn of God and righteousness in his Word and because Jesus Christ affirmed the authority of all Scripture (Matthew 24:35; John 10:35; 14:26), a believer should have no problem knowing where to land on virtually all ethical issues.

This is why we may assert that, regarding issues of morality, our conclusions are informed by our relationship to our Savior and Lord, Jesus Christ. In John 17:17, Jesus prayed to the Father, saying, "Sanctify them by Your truth. Your word is truth." God's Word, the Bible, is our source of divine truth. Paul wrote in 2 Timothy 3:16–17, "All Scripture is given by inspiration of God, and is profitable for doctrine, for reproof, for correction, for instruction in righteousness, that the man of God may be complete, thoroughly equipped for every good work." The words *inspiration of God* translate literally as "God-breathed" in Greek, meaning Scripture is an extension of God himself. Rightly interpreted, Scripture is God's truth on all issues of morality.

A person can have a personal preference, but you cannot have a "personal truth." God defines right and wrong in Scripture for us to learn and obey, not for us to pick and choose. Writer Paul Copan noted the following:

> Something can be true even if no one knows it.
> Something can be true even if no one admits it.
> Something can be true even if no one agrees what it is.
> Something can be true even if no one follows it.
> Something can be true even if no one but God grasps it fully.[5]

---

5 Paul Copan, *True for You, But Not for Me: Overcoming Objections to Christian Faith*, rev. ed. (Bloomington, MN: Bethany House, 2009), 20.

If a person has cancer, they want the correct diagnosis and the best doctor to fight it. The same should be true when it comes to spiritual matters. We want the correct diagnosis of the problem of sin in our lives and the best solution for it. The Bible clearly identifies morality and the Great Physician who can heal us from our sin problem.

Some also argue that we can't believe in God for truth because we can't see him. This is a false accusation, as we regularly accept facts that we do not fully understand or cannot see. When we fly in an airplane, we accept that rules are in place to safely help us arrive at our destination. When we eat at a restaurant, we accept that the food will not contain deadly poison because of laws that are in place to enforce safe conditions. With God, we can trust his promises because he is perfect. He does not lie, nor does he deceive us. Instead, he loves us and has revealed truth to us through his Word and through his Son Jesus Christ.

43. HOW CAN I KNOW THE TEACHINGS OF CHRISTIANITY ARE REAL?

Many have wondered how Christianity can be real. Our answer to anyone with doubts about Christianity is to investigate it. The Christian faith is the only religion we have been able to investigate and repeatedly verify as accurate based on the facts of history. The Bible does include many supernatural activities, but there is also evidence to support many of Scripture's accounts.

The greatest fact in favor of Christianity is simply the empty tomb. The enemies of Jesus could not produce his body to disprove the resurrection. The Jews claimed that the disciples of Jesus stole the body. However, according to church tradition, all but one of the eleven disciples (excluding Judas Iscariot, who betrayed Jesus) died for their faith. It seems clear that if someone had supported a lie or conspiracy theory, he would have eventually confessed. Instead, no one ever found the body, and millions of people have experienced changed lives through the teachings of Christ.

Another area that supports the truth of Christianity is archaeology. Archaeologists have made thousands of historical discoveries that support the teachings and facts of the Bible. Still today, the Western Wall of the Jewish temple remains standing, offering clear evidence of the temple's existence and importance in both Judaism and early Christianity. Cities like Jerusalem, Nineveh, Hebron, Ephesus, and many others have been verified. Nearly every part of Israel contains remains that highlight the history of the Jewish people and biblical history.

The evidence of the Bible also supports Christianity. More than fifty-eight hundred handwritten ancient copies of the New Testament exist, far more than any other writing from antiquity. Many experts have made comparisons among these copies to ensure accurate preservation of the text, revealing both the accuracy of the Scriptures and the power of God to protect his Word despite efforts to destroy it throughout history.

A fourth area that we find fascinating is fulfilled prophecy. Many Bible prophecies were later fulfilled with stunning accuracy, especially those related to Jesus. He was born of a virgin, which Isaiah 7:14 predicted seven hundred years earlier. Jesus also came as the suffering Messiah, also predicted by Isaiah in chapter 53. Micah 5:2 predicted the Messiah's birth in Bethlehem, and Psalm 22 clearly describes the death of Jesus on the cross.

A fifth area that we can also observe is the changed lives of people. Well-known writers like C. S. Lewis and Lee Strobel have shared their personal testimonies of how Jesus changed them. Millions of other people have seen the power of God change their lives, restore their families, break their addictions, and heal their relationships.

While we could add other areas, the empty tomb, archaeology, the Bible, fulfilled prophecy, and changed lives all point toward the truth of Christianity, not away from it. We can investigate Christianity without fear, knowing that such study will strengthen our faith in the Lord.

44. HOW DO I OVERCOME A BAD HABIT OR SIN IN MY LIFE?

We all have areas of sin or bad habits in our lives that we would like to change, but how can we make progress? What does God's Word say to help?

First, we must recognize the fact that developing a bad habit includes our thoughts as part of the temptation process. James 1:14–15 teaches, "Each one is tempted when he is drawn away by his own desires and enticed. Then, when desire has conceived, it gives birth to sin; and sin, when it is full-grown, brings forth death." If we can identify the desire that tempts us, we may be able to remove it or at least see it coming in time to stop it.

Second, we pray. As with all things, prayer can create supernatural change in ways other actions cannot. Never forget the power of prayer in the process of change. It's ultimately God at work in us to create change and not our own efforts.

Third, replace bad habits with good ones. For example, one man said that he was tempted to look at inappropriate things online on his phone at night. To help, he would turn on his audio Bible app and listen to Scripture while he was online. He noticed it was difficult to go to an inappropriate website while listening to God's Word. This is a great example of putting off "the old man" like Paul mentioned in Ephesians 4:22–24: "Put off, concerning your former conduct, the old man which grows corrupt according to the deceitful lusts, and be renewed in the spirit of your mind, and that you put on the new man which was created according to God, in true righteousness and holiness."

Fourth, dedicate your time to living for God. Romans 12:1–2 says, "I beseech you therefore, brethren, by the mercies of God, that you present your bodies a living sacrifice, holy, acceptable to God, which is your reasonable service. And do not be conformed to this world, but be transformed by the renewing of your mind, that you may prove what is that good and acceptable and perfect will of God." When we focus our life around God and his priorities, we have less time to be tempted to do wrong. This includes meditating on God's Word. Psalm 1:1–2 says, "Blessed is the man who walks not in the counsel of the ungodly, nor stands in the path of sinners, nor sits in the seat of the scornful; but his delight is in the law of the Lord, and in His law he meditates day and night." If we want to be blessed, one clear way is to focus time each day on God's Word as our source of wisdom and strength.

Fifth, surround yourself with godly friends. The wrong kind of friends will increase temptation because they are likely to also participate in your sinful actions or behaviors or at least support you when you do. Godly friends will encourage you to do what is right and help you in your times of weakness. Just one good Christian friend can make a tremendous impact.

Sixth, in some cases you may need to consider professional help. It is not wrong to seek help from a minister or professional counselor if you have a serious problem or addiction. For too long, many Christians have treated professional counseling as evil or as a weakness, but there are times when you may need more dedicated help than your friends can provide or than you can give yourself.

45. WHAT DOES THE BIBLE SAY ABOUT OUR USE OF
MEDIA (VIDEO GAMES, MOVIES, TELEVISION, SOCIAL
MEDIA)?

Video games and movies didn't exist during biblical times. Does Scripture give us any guidelines for how to handle these areas of life? We believe it does. God promised, "His divine power hath given unto us all things that pertain unto life and godliness, through the knowledge of him that hath called us to glory and virtue" (2 Peter 1:3 KJV). It's important to recognize that video games, movies, television, and even social media are forms of communication and art. They both inform culture and form culture. They reflect what is happening and shape what happens in the future. They can be used for both good and evil. It's up to us to recognize the benefits and concerns involved and to address them from a biblical worldview. We don't advocate that people throw away their computers or phones or televisions, but at times, we need to set limits to protect our hearts.

First, it's also important to evaluate the content we are consuming. A good question to ask yourself is, *If Jesus were in the room, would he watch this video or show with me?* If the answer is no or if you would be embarrassed if he saw you, we recommend reevaluating what you're watching. You can also consider using filters to block violence and pornography. Ultimately, God is with you whether you are aware of it or not. If you have children, you are also responsible for guarding what they see and hear as well as how much they see and hear. This is now a time-consuming effort, as many companies have chosen to include inappropriate content for younger viewers. Always remember that your children look to you as an example of how to consume media in a God-honoring way.

Second, consider the impact your use of media has on other people. For example, many Americans, especially men, enjoy watching football and other sports for hours at a time. Sports are great, but the amount of time and energy we invest in these activities can keep us from other areas God wants us to pursue, including building relationships and serving others. Our media usage may also distract other people from their daily activities and God's purposes for them, especially if we use our devices in public spaces with loud volumes or flashing lights. We should always ask ourselves whether the way we consume media pleases the Lord and set time limits regarding how long we use our devices.

Third, give priority to the people physically with you. Our devices now often turn us into "phone zombies" who walk and look down without talking to or even noticing one another. Smartphones, tablets, and computers also complicate our efforts as they make it convenient to play games and watch videos at any time, even during meals. It's sad to see a family eating together at a restaurant when every person is on a device without talking to one another. Also, it has sadly become increasingly necessary to tell kids (and some adults) to stop texting or gaming during church services. While we are happy whenever people attend church, we want them fully there and focused on the things of God for their spiritual development. Choose to invest your attention in those with you and watch how God uses the time together to grow your in-person relationships.

Fourth, don't forget to take a break from technology and media consumption. Did you know that practicing Jews today turn off all their devices when observing the Sabbath? It seems like a radical move to many of us, but it offers a powerful example of the need to take regular breaks from our media to focus on the Lord.

If you're overwhelmed by the media you or those in your family are consuming, try some of these ideas to take back control of the media that seeks to control us and watch how God works in your relationship with him and with others.

46. WHAT DOES THE BIBLE TEACH ABOUT SOCIAL JUSTICE?

Social justice has become the rallying cry of some people and an evil term for others. What is it, and how should we address social justice as Christians?

Social justice is the popular term people use to address issues of humanitarian or social need in our culture. For example, feeding the poor can be a form of social justice, but some people also use the phrase to advocate for open borders or even increased abortion access, complicating the use of the term among Christians.

God is certainly in favor of justice, but a biblical worldview does not include everything today's social justice warrior would include. Instead of social justice, we advocate for Christians to stand for biblical justice. More specifically, it is important to define our convictions on particular issues rather than blindly accepting any topic on today's highly political social justice agenda.

We can certainly agree that feeding the poor, providing clean water, helping with disaster relief, and many other activities are Christian efforts we desire to support. In addition, there are other areas that Christians care about, like opposing discrimination or helping immigrants, but Christians may address these issues differently than non-Christians who promote social justice. By ensuring we serve in ways that honor God and align with the Bible, we can more accurately and appropriately respond to the needs of our culture.

In some ways, social justice seems to simply be trying to make community service into something political. Christians have always been called to love our neighbor as ourselves and to treat others the way we would like to be treated. When traditionally helpful actions become parts of political agendas supporting areas inconsistent with our biblical worldview, we need to clearly take a stand on what is and isn't acceptable for our participation.

What about those who argue that Jesus advocated for social justice? Didn't he overturn the tables in the temple and oppose evil in his earthly ministry? He did, but we shouldn't take these examples out of context and apply them to areas Jesus opposed.

Christians must also be careful to avoid violent protests, even when supporting causes that align with a biblical worldview. For example, even though God certainly opposes both abortion and discrimination against people based on their ethnicity or race, we are not called to participate in violence to advocate against abortion or racism. The apostle Paul taught we are to speak the truth in love (see Ephesians 4:15), focusing on the good news of Jesus and its power to change lives.

In practical terms, this means we should still advocate for areas of social justice that help people in biblical ways but should not blindly participate in social justice activities that could oppose our convictions. The gospel is our focus, and showing Christ's love is the goal. When we focus on serving others based on our biblical worldview, we can take a Good Samaritan approach that changes lives and shows the love of Jesus in appropriate ways.

47. WHAT IS A CHRISTIAN VIEW OF SPORTS AND PHYSICAL TRAINING?

Our world greatly emphasizes the importance of sports and physical training. While it was once rare to see youth sports played on Sundays, it is now common to have children missing from church because they are on traveling sports teams. Multiple television channels stream sports twenty-four seven while a countless number of websites, leagues, fantasy sports, and even sports betting continue to grow as a multibillion-dollar industry.

A biblical look at sports and physical activity should cause us some concern regarding the tremendous cultural emphasis on these activities. Fitness and athletic activity offer many positive benefits, but they are limited in comparison with a focus on godly living. Paul wrote the key biblical teaching on this topic in 1 Timothy 4:8-11: "For bodily exercise profits a little, but godliness is profitable for all things, having promise of the life that now is and of that which is to come. This is a faithful saying and worthy of all acceptance. For to this end we both labor and suffer reproach, because we trust in the living God, who is the Savior of all men, especially of those who believe. These things command and teach."

First, this verse shows that physical training is valuable, but its benefits are limited. Our culture often emphasizes building big muscles, having six-pack abs, or being the star of a sports team as the top goals of life. God says physical training is of some benefit, but it doesn't compare with living for the Lord.

Second, godliness is "profitable for all things." In contrast to sports or lifting weights or running, godly training has an eternal impact. Training ourselves spiritually affects our life, the lives of those around us, and even our eternal rewards.

Third, godliness is worth pursuing with greater intensity than physical training. What if we pursued God as much as we did our sports? Instead of a travel league for our children, perhaps we could take our kids to Christian events to help them grow in their faith. Instead of watching another game, maybe we could pray more or serve someone in need.

Again, sports are positive, but putting sports above God is not. It has been said that if someone who had never experienced our culture were shown a football or basketball stadium, they would likely conclude that the fans were worshiping the ball or the players. We cheer for them, dress for them, and dedicate much time and money to them. We can easily focus too much on our favorite team or player or sport—or even on our own involvement in playing a sport—in ways that damage our time serving the Lord.

When it comes to priorities, where do you draw the line? Take a serious look at your focus on sports and physical activities, and make sure your life lines up with Scripture's teachings when it comes to keeping God first and sports lower on the list.

48. SHOULD I HAVE MY CHILDREN ATTEND PUBLIC SCHOOL, GO TO A CHRISTIAN SCHOOL, OR BE HOMESCHOOLED?

Where your child attends school is a critical decision that you should make with much prayer and consideration. How can you decide whether your child should attend a public school, a Christian school, or be homeschooled?

The Bible offers guidelines to help. First, Scripture is clear that parents hold the primary responsibility for the education of their children: "Train up a child in the way he should go: and when he is old, he will not depart from it" (Proverbs 22:6 KJV). You must decide the form of schooling your child receives, not the government or the society in which you live.

Let's consider the positives and negatives of each option. A public school is often the only available choice when no Christian school exists in the area and parents must work during the school day. The benefits include taxpayer-funded resources, social activities and sports, and connections with other children in the community. The negatives can vary widely among schools and usually relate to school safety and the moral issues our children face. For example, some schools have become increasingly progressive and have sought to normalize some perspectives that are not biblical. Parents must be careful to stay involved and aware of these potential concerns at the local level.

For a Christian school, the benefits usually include the biblical worldview presented in the classroom, the involvement of Christian teachers, students, coaches, and parents, as well as smaller classes and more personalized attention, which are common in private schools. The negatives of Christian education are twofold. The major issue is the high price of private education. Many parents are unable to consider the option from a financial standpoint. The second common concern is that isolating a child in a Christian environment sometimes offers an unrealistic view of the world that leaves a student unprepared for life after graduation.

Homeschooling has perhaps been the fastest-growing form of education over the past two decades. While nearly every parent was forced into some home-schooling during the COVID-19 pandemic, a growing number of parents have chosen this option for a variety of reasons. Some of these reasons include more time with children, personalized learning, less stress and social pressure, safety, health reasons, and more flexibility in scheduling. However, homeschooling provides children fewer opportunities to bond with other children their age and does require the commitment of both parents, often requiring a family to live on one income, which may not be financially possible. Many homeschool families balance the social needs of children by joining homeschool sports leagues, participating in church activities, and hosting collective activities with other homeschoolers in foreign languages, music, dance, and the arts.

We want to encourage you to stay involved in your child's education as much as possible, regardless of the option you feel led to choose. Not everyone can homeschool, but those who can consider it a rewarding experience that offers much additional time with their children. Christian schools can offer great resources and a flourishing environment for those able to access and afford the option. Public schools offer deep community connections as well as ministry opportunities to reach children and adults, though parents must exercise much caution in exposing their children to a secular environment.

It is also important that believers in the local church work together as a team to build one another up, and believers are called to respect each family's schooling choice without condemning their decision. Unless the decision involves a violation of a clear biblical principle, we are called to encourage one another in biblical community to help families and children grow in the Lord and in their educational pursuits.

49. How do I keep my child or grandchild from losing faith while in college?

One of the deepest concerns of many parents and grandparents is that their children or grandchildren will lose their faith in college. After eighteen years of raising a child to love God and other people, it's disheartening when a young adult abandons the teachings of their faith. What can be done to help?

First, realize you're not alone if this is your situation. Every parent, grandparent, pastor, and youth leader shares the concern of helping the next generation remain faithful during their early adult years.

Second, we've recognized that the best defense against secularization is a deep and early foundation. It's one thing to take your child to church or a children's ministry or youth group. It's much different when your child sees you personally praying, reading Scripture, and applying biblical principles to your life. Your children are much more likely to copy what they see you do every day over what they see for an hour or two at church each week. This area also includes establishing habits for your children. Don't just have your children attend church. Help them serve in the church, practice a regular prayer and Bible reading time, and build deep connections with other believers throughout their childhood in whatever situation God has placed you. When children look back at their childhood faith, these positive memories and habits will remind them of the importance of living out their faith during difficult times.

Third, community is key. If your child is heading to a college campus away from home, make it a priority to connect them with other Christians, a local church, and Christian groups at their university. Each college has a list of student organizations that will most likely include one or more options. When your children have other friends doing the right thing, they are more likely to do so as well. This also includes local church involvement. In addition to other Christian college students, your children need people of all ages who love God to share in a weekly routine. Helping your college-aged student find a church home, even if it's different from their childhood church, is a critical factor in a student remaining faithful in their walk with the Lord.

These principles are also true if your adult child is not attending college or is serving in the military or another role. Take up the challenge of helping connect your children to other Christians wherever they are, along with churches and ministries that could help them thrive in their faith.

Fourth, recognize that you don't graduate from parenting. Your children may graduate high school at the age of eighteen, but this doesn't necessarily make them a fully independent adult. Your role may change, but it is not over. Stay involved in ways that help by praying for your child, staying in contact, and continuing your relationship to help them stay on God's path.

Fifth, know that even if your child does turn against their faith at some point, that is not the end of the story. The account of the prodigal son in Luke 15 clearly illustrates that a person's rebellion can later become a rebound that brings them home. If your child strays, be like the father in Luke 15:20: "When he was yet a great way off, his father saw him, and had compassion, and ran, and fell on his neck, and kissed him" (KJV). The father was waiting and ready to accept his son back, celebrating his son's return. This does not mean we let a rebellious adult child mistreat our kindness, but it clearly supports the idea that we should foster an ongoing love for our children and a willingness to give them another chance even after they have made mistakes.

50. HOW CAN CHRISTIANS CLAIM TO BE PRO-LIFE AND STILL SUPPORT THE DEATH PENALTY?

A common accusation by proabortion advocates is that Christians are not really pro-life if they support the death penalty. Is this true?

Not exactly. First, these are two separate issues. Abortion proponents may often use unrelated issues like the death penalty to distract or justify their own views rather than to express genuine concern regarding those facing the death penalty.

Second, the death penalty, at least in the United States, is limited to those convicted of first-degree murder and exists only in certain states. If a person has intentionally murdered someone else, then seeking the death penalty is not in opposition to a pro-life position. It is a defense against those who are pro-death.

Third, a biblical look at life in the womb and the death penalty reveals that a follower of the Lord can support both the pro-life view and capital punishment. In brief, the pro-life view is built on beliefs that include acknowledging God as the creator of all life (Genesis 1:27), accepting that God puts us together in the womb (Psalm 139:13), and trusting that he has a purpose for our life from the womb (Jeremiah 1:5).

Support for the death penalty can be based on a variety of biblical principles. In the Jewish law, capital punishment was required for premeditated murder but was also required in many other cases, including some we would not agree with today, such as gathering firewood on the Sabbath day (Numbers 15:32–36). In the New Testament, the apostle Paul urged believers to submit to governing authorities in Romans 13. Verse 4 notes, "He is God's minister to you for good. But if you do evil, be afraid; for he does not bear the sword in vain; for he is God's minister, an avenger to execute wrath on him who practices evil." In other words, Paul assumed the validity of capital punishment, arguing that those who are law-abiding citizens do not need to live in fear of punishment. Keep in mind that Paul wrote this even though he would later personally be put to death for his faith, according to church tradition.

The Bible does not require capital punishment for murder, however. The first murder recorded in the Bible was Cain killing his brother Abel. God punished Cain with banishment, but the Lord did not put him to death. King David had Uriah, the husband of Bathsheba, put to death. God judged David and his kingdom but did not kill him over it.

According to Scripture, a Christian worldview demands a pro-life view that opposes abortion. When it comes to the death penalty, the Bible includes it as one option but not as a requirement. Those who seek to make a false connection between the two are not doing so based on biblical principles but largely to push the concept to support a proabortion perspective.

SECTION 7

NEW TESTAMENT QUESTIONS

51. IF JESUS IS GOD, HOW COULD HE BE TEMPTED BY SATAN?

Many have asked how Jesus could be tempted by Satan in the wilderness if Jesus is God. The key to understanding the context of Christ's temptation is found in understanding that Jesus is both fully God and fully human. Yes, he is and always has been divine. However, he was also born of a woman, grew in his human body, and experienced the highs and lows of living as a person in our world, including the temptations we face.

In Matthew 4:1–11 and Luke 4:1–13, we read about Jesus fasting for forty days in the wilderness and being tempted on three occasions by Satan. Matthew 4:2 says Jesus was hungry. Verse 3 adds that "the tempter came to Him." The devil sought to use the human emotions Jesus was feeling to cause him to sin. Instead of sinning, Jesus resisted, quoting God's Word to stop Satan's attempt. Jesus did this on two other occasions, with the devil leaving without success to end the account. The verses portray Jesus as human but also as divine as he conquered the temptations of the devil.

In one example, when Jesus responded to Satan's third attempt in Luke 4:12, he said, "You shall not tempt the Lord your God." These words are key. Jesus, who is God the Son, condemned Satan's temptation by using Scripture that highlighted Jesus' divine nature. James 1:13 later adds, "Let no one say when he is tempted, 'I am tempted by God'; for God cannot be tempted by evil, nor does He Himself tempt anyone." Jesus proved himself to be God by not sinning when tempted.

Here is a question we might ponder in relation to all of this: Was Satan aware that Jesus, the Son of God, could not or would not sin while here on earth? Satan obviously thought that Jesus *would* fall into sin (and was, therefore, unqualified to be the world's Messiah). It stands to reason that Satan wouldn't have wasted his time on the wilderness temptations had he thought it impossible for Jesus to sin.

The author of Hebrews built on the importance of Christ's sinless nature: "We do not have a High Priest who cannot sympathize with our weaknesses, but was in all points tempted as we are, yet without sin. Let us therefore come boldly to the throne of grace, that we may obtain mercy and find grace to help in time of need" (4:15–16). Jesus was tempted just like we are but did not sin. His strength to resist all sin can help us when we turn to him in our time of need through prayer and dependence.

Even when Jesus endured the scorn and pain of death on the cross, he refused to sin. Philippians 2:8–9 observes, "And being found in appearance as a man, He humbled Himself and became obedient to the point of death, even the death of the cross. Therefore God also has highly exalted Him and given Him the name which is above every name." His humility in the face of suffering and temptation contrasts with his greatness as King of kings and Lord of lords.

Jesus was tempted in his human nature yet resisted all temptation due to his divine nature. He proved that despite his human body, he is, has been, and always will be the perfect Son of God, the second person of triune Godhead.

52. WHAT DID JESUS DO BETWEEN THE AGES OF ABOUT TWELVE AND THIRTY?

Many questions surround the early life of Jesus. The gospel writers describe his birth along with an incident from when he was twelve years old. The next time we read about Jesus, he is about thirty years old. What did Jesus do between these ages?

Joseph and Mary accidentally lost Jesus during a trip to Jerusalem when Jesus was twelve years old (Luke 2:41–50). The account concludes with the words, "Then He went down with them and came to Nazareth, and was subject to them, but His mother kept all these things in her heart. And Jesus increased in wisdom and stature, and in favor with God and men" (vv. 51–52). It appears that Jesus continued to live in Nazareth, where he likely learned Joseph's profession of carpentry while also learning the Hebrew traditions of his faith.

When we discover Jesus again in the next chapter of Luke, John the Baptist is baptizing him in the Jordan River. Scripture also notes that Jesus is still close with his mother, Mary, and that he apparently had four brothers (James, Joses, Simon, and Judas/Jude) and at least two sisters (Matthew 13:54–56). People knew him as being from Nazareth, meaning Jesus likely lived there until his ministry at about the age of thirty.

Two of his brothers, James and Jude, would later write the letters of the New Testament that bear their names. Mary was also a leader in the early church. But what about Joseph? He was not mentioned when Jesus started his public ministry, indicating Joseph may have passed away during these years. If so, it would also explain why Jesus, the oldest son, remained in Nazareth where he could help his mother, a responsibility he would later pass on to his disciple John (John 19:25–27).

There is also a fictional account of the childhood of Jesus. An early writing called the Infancy Gospel of Thomas (likely from the second century) describes activities in the life of Jesus between the ages of five and twelve. The account includes several miracles, including turning clay into living birds, an act also cited in the Islamic holy book of the Qur'an (5:110).

Other miracles in the so-called Gospel of Thomas include Jesus healing his brother James from a venomous snake along with resurrecting both a child and a man who died in a work accident. Is there any evidence that these events occurred? Not really. The activities are not mentioned in the New Testament and only arose in later generations when a growing number of fictional accounts about Jesus began to appear. In addition, the late date of the writing and lack of connection to earlier apostolic material point to a form of writing rooted in fiction apart from the historical traditions of the early church.

Instead, the Bible focuses on the miraculous aspects of Christ's birth, his prophetic fulfillments, and then on his ministry as an adult. The gospel accounts were not written as a detailed biography but instead include writings led by the Holy Spirit, who inspired the writers to emphasize the aspects of central importance of those who follow Jesus.

53. WHAT HAPPENED TO JOSEPH, THE EARTHLY FATHER OF JESUS?

Joseph was the husband of Mary, Jesus' mother, and he raised Jesus as his son. He was known as a carpenter from Nazareth from the family of David in Bethlehem, yet he is not mentioned during the ministry of Jesus. What happened to him?

The Bible does not explicitly say what happened to Joseph. Outside of his role during the birth and infancy of Jesus, we only know a few details regarding Joseph.

First, he was still alive when Jesus was twelve years old because Jesus traveled with Joseph and Mary to Jerusalem at that time.

Second, Joseph was the father of four boys and at least two girls. Matthew 13:55–56 reveals people in the synagogue of Nazareth saying, "Is this not the carpenter's son? Is not His mother called Mary? And His brothers James, Joses, Simon, and Judas? And His sisters, are they not all with us?"

Third, people who knew Jesus referred to him as "the carpenter's son." Joseph likely continued to serve in his trade for his entire life.

Fourth, in John 2:1, we read that Mary was at a wedding, but Joseph is not mentioned. It would have been highly unlikely for her to attend a wedding without her husband if he were still alive. Instead, Jesus was there with her along with some of his disciples.

Fifth, Jesus handed over the responsibility of caring for his mother to his disciple John. Jesus would not likely have done this if his own father were still alive. It appears Jesus, as the oldest son, was already the one responsible for his mother after Joseph's death and was passing on the role to John shortly before Jesus' own death on the cross. Some have also noted that Joseph would have been responsible for burying the body of Jesus after his death if Joseph were still alive.

Regarding more details about the life and death of Joseph, this is an example of the Bible providing everything we *need* to know but not necessarily telling us all things we'd *like* to know. Some traditions suggest Joseph died prior to the start of the ministry of Jesus, but accounts outside of Scripture are speculative. Another consideration is Joseph's age compared to the average life span of men during the first century in Israel. For example, if Joseph was in his twenties at the birth of Jesus, he would have been around fifty or older at the time Jesus began his ministry. A Middle Eastern man dying at this age would not have been surprising during that time period. Mary may have been several years younger than Joseph, a common cultural practice at that time, which would have been partly responsible for her living several years longer than her husband.

We are not told when or how Joseph died. Perhaps Joseph passed away within a few years of Jesus starting his ministry. If so, he would have been buried in Nazareth, known as a carpenter who played a key role in the life of Jesus in the New Testament. Beyond what Scripture states explicitly, we simply don't know.

54. If Jesus was already perfect, why did John the Baptist baptize him?

Jesus began his public ministry by being baptized by John the Baptist. Why did Jesus need to be baptized if he had not sinned?

Scripture reveals several significant reasons for this important event. First, the baptism revealed to John that the Messiah had come. In John 1:26–27, John the Baptist predicted, "I baptize with water, but there stands One among you whom you do not know. It is He who, coming after me, is preferred before me, whose sandal strap I am not worthy to loose." When Jesus appeared the next day, God revealed to John that Jesus was the Lamb of God, and John said, "Behold! The Lamb of God who takes away the sin of the world! This is He of whom I said, 'After me comes a Man who is preferred before me, for He was before me.' I did not know Him; but that He should be revealed to Israel, therefore I came baptizing with water" (vv. 29–31).

Second, Jesus was baptized to "fulfill all righteousness." John and Matthew both recorded the baptism of Jesus. The phrase used in Matthew 3:15 served as part of fulfilling the predictions of the coming Messiah: "Permit it to be so now, for thus it is fitting for us to fulfill all righteousness."

Third, the baptism of Jesus marked the first account in the New Testament of all three persons of the triune God appearing together in the same account. Matthew 3:16–17 says, "Jesus, when he was baptized, went up straightway out of the water: and, lo, the heavens were opened unto him, and he saw the Spirit of God descending like a dove, and lighting upon him: and lo a voice from heaven, saying, This is my beloved Son, in whom I am well pleased" (KJV). Jesus, the Holy Spirit, and the voice of God the Father were all present and acting at the same time.

Fourth, Jesus was baptized as an example for his followers. Jesus began his public ministry with his own baptism. He ended his earthly ministry with a call for his followers to baptize others: "Go therefore and make disciples of all the nations, baptizing them in the name of the Father and of the Son and of the Holy Spirit, teaching them to observe all things that I have commanded you; and lo, I am with you always, even to the end of the age" (Matthew 28:19–20). Many, including us, also agree that the baptism of Jesus highlights the importance of the baptism of believers by immersion. Jesus was baptized in the water of the Jordan River. He called his followers in the Great Commission to baptize others when they became disciples.

The baptism of Jesus was not necessary as a sign of his public profession of faith or due to any sins he had committed. Instead, his baptism fulfilled prophecy, revealed God in a unique way, and set an example for those who would believe in and follow him. The apostle Peter clearly noted that baptism is "not the removal of the filth of the flesh, but the answer of a good conscience toward God" (1 Peter 3:21) for those who trust in the Lord Jesus Christ.

55. WHY DID JESUS SAY, "BLESSED ARE THOSE WHO MOURN" (MATTHEW 5:4)?

In the Sermon on the Mount, a section known as the Beatitudes includes the phrase, "Blessed are those who mourn" (Matthew 5:4). How can mourning lead to blessing?

A look at the context of this teaching offers much insight into this question. The phrase is the second in a series of blessings Jesus gives. In the previous verse, Jesus contrasted the poor in spirit with the kingdom of heaven. In this verse, he said those who mourn will be blessed because they will be comforted. In other words, those who follow the Lord will not face sadness without hope. Jesus pointed to a future time when his people would experience comfort from their mourning, turning their pain into a blessing.

When believers mourn over sin, God raises them up and restores them to fruitful living. A powerful example of mourning over sin is found in the life of David. After he sinned in his relationship with Bathsheba and in setting up her husband, Uriah, to die in battle, he mourned his sin (Psalm 51). In verses 2–3, David urged the Lord, "Wash me thoroughly from my iniquity, and cleanse me from my sin. For I acknowledge my transgressions, and my sin is always before me."

The apostle Paul also addressed the relationship between mourning in this life and the joy of being with the Lord and with other believers in eternity: "I do not want you to be ignorant, brethren, concerning those who have fallen asleep, lest you sorrow as others who have no hope. For if we believe that Jesus died and rose again, even so God will bring with Him those who sleep in Jesus" (1 Thessalonians 4:13–14).

Paul also described an account in 2 Corinthians 5:16–21 in which mourning led to repentance. Verse 17 says, "Therefore, if anyone is in Christ, he is a new creation; old things have passed away; behold, all things have become new." When we come to faith in the Lord, we become a new creation, and our sins are forgiven. This freedom brings great joy to those who have received his salvation.

Those who listened to Peter preach on the day of Pentecost also mourned in a way that led to repentance and salvation: "When they heard this, they were pricked in their heart, and said unto Peter and to the rest of the apostles, Men and brethren, what shall we do?" (Acts 2:37 KJV).

This new life in Christ is also an ongoing part of our daily walk with God. We experience joy when we come to know the Lord, and we can rejoice each day as we faithfully walk with him. The apostle Peter wrote, "Though now you do not see Him, yet believing, you rejoice with joy inexpressible and full of glory, receiving the end of your faith—the salvation of your souls" (1 Peter 1:8–9).

Mourning is part of living in a fallen world. We mourn when we grieve the loss of a loved one or experience other pains in life. However, we also have hope within us through our faith in Jesus Christ that gives us a blessing that endures both now and for eternity. Colossians 1:27 refers to this joy as "Christ in you, the hope of glory."

56. WHY DID JESUS SAY HEAVEN WOULD PASS AWAY (MATTHEW 24:35)?

The Bible is clear that the earth's time is limited and will one day fade away, but what about heaven? Why did Jesus teach that heaven would also pass away? Isn't this the home of believers for all eternity?

Let's take a closer look at this often-confusing topic. In Matthew 24:35, Jesus spoke of the future, telling his disciples, "Heaven and earth shall pass away, but my words shall not pass away" (KJV). Jesus affirmed both that his words are eternal and that the world, including heaven, is temporary. He also mentioned this passing away in Matthew 5:18. Matthew 24:36 says this will take place at the end of time at a moment that no one knows. Jesus was referring to when he will ultimately end everything as we now know it and create a new heaven and new earth. A glimpse of the new heaven and earth is described in Revelation 21 and 22, the last two chapters of the Bible.

Revelation 22:1–3 offer part of the amazing setting that one day awaits all believers: "He showed me a pure river of water of life, clear as crystal, proceeding from the throne of God and of the Lamb. In the middle of its street, and on either side of the river, was the tree of life, which bore twelve fruits, each tree yielding its fruit every month. The leaves of the tree were for the healing of the nations. And there shall be no more curse, but the throne of God and of the Lamb shall be in it, and His servants shall serve Him."

When will this take place? Revelation 21:1 indicates that this new heaven will replace the previous one: "I saw a new heaven and a new earth, for the first heaven and the first earth had passed away." The future outline will include Christ's coming at the rapture, the seven-year tribulation, the return of Christ to earth with his people, his millennial reign, a final fight against Satan and those with him, and judgment upon Satan before the new period begins.

What does that mean for the timeline of heaven? Believers who pass away now are immediately in the presence of the Lord. Paul wrote in Philippians 1:23 that he wanted "a desire to depart, and to be with Christ; which is far better" (KJV). His words confirm that we are immediately in the Lord's presence after this life. It appears that all believers will leave the current heaven and join Christ at his second coming as described in Revelation 19. We will then live with him in the millennial kingdom (see 20:1-6) until he creates the new heaven and earth, where we will dwell with him forever.

Heaven will last forever, but even our eternal home will be made new in the end, offering a perfect eternal home for all of God's people. As 2 Peter 3:13 says, "We, according to His promise, look for new heavens and a new earth in which righteousness dwells."

57. WHAT DOES THE WORD *PRODIGAL* MEAN IN THE STORY OF THE PRODIGAL SON?

The story of the prodigal son in Luke 15 is one of the most powerful examples Jesus provided of the love between God the Father and those who turn to him. But *prodigal* is not a word many of us use in our daily lives. What does it mean to be a prodigal child? What is the importance of this word in the account told by Jesus?

In English, *prodigal* can be defined as a person who spends money in a reckless or extravagant way. The Prodigal Son refers to the younger son in the story found in Luke 15:11-32 and the lifestyle he chose. The son received an early inheritance from his father. Verses 13-14 explain, "Not many days after, the younger son gathered all together, journeyed to a far country, and there wasted his possessions with prodigal living. But when he had spent all, there arose a severe famine in that land, and he began to be in want." The word *prodigal* is used in verse 13 to refer to his wild and wasteful lifestyle. Instead of investing his inheritance wisely, he quickly lost it through his pursuit of pleasure.

The Prodigal Son soon hit a low point, working to feed pigs and craving the food eaten by the animals. Under Jewish law, pigs were unclean animals, making the situation even more humiliating. This low point led the Prodigal Son to reflect on his situation and consider a return to his father. Even his father's workers ate and lived better than he did now. The son chose to humble himself and work for his father rather than remain in his situation. How would his father respond? "When he was still a great way off, his father saw him and had compassion, and ran and fell on his neck and kissed him," verse 20 reads. It appears his father was eagerly anticipating his son's return. He welcomed his son home with a celebration, saying, "This my son was dead and is alive again; he was lost and is found" (v. 24).

Many people stop the story at this point, but Jesus continued with the response of the older son. This older son was angry because while he had faithfully served his father, the wasteful younger son was the one receiving a celebration. The father expressed his gratitude to his older son but also emphasized the importance of receiving the son who had returned home. "It was right that we should make merry and be glad, for your brother was dead and is alive again, and was lost and is found" (v. 32). Likewise, we often find ourselves envious of how God blesses someone else who turns to him after a sinful background when we believe we have been faithful for much longer. Instead, we are called to rejoice with those who turn to God, celebrating the prodigals among us who return to the Lord. Just as the heavenly Father receives those who trust in him, he calls us to love and encourage those of all backgrounds who come to the Lord.

58. Should Christians observe the Sabbath?

The Sabbath is an important biblical concept, but it is often confusing for Christians today. What is it, and should Christians observe the Sabbath today?

First, the Sabbath is the seventh day in the Jewish calendar, which is on Saturday. God created the heavens and the earth in six days and rested on the seventh day. It technically begins Friday at sunset and ends Saturday at sunset.

Second, the Jewish law included strict teachings regarding the Sabbath. After four hundred years of slavery in Egypt, the Lord commanded his people to rest every seventh day and do no work. The Sabbath was such a central part of Jewish culture that it was included as one of the Ten Commandments.

Third, practicing Jews continue to observe the Sabbath today. If you were to visit Israel, for example, much of the nation still stops operating from sunset Friday until sunset Saturday. Some variations occur in how people in other parts of the world practice the Sabbath rest.

Fourth, church history has often complicated the Sabbath by claiming that the Sabbath "switched" to Sunday after the resurrection of Jesus. While Sunday is traditionally known as the Lord's Day and is celebrated as the first day of the week, the day when Jesus rose from the dead, that does not mean the Sabbath has changed days. Early Jewish Christians observed the Sabbath and then worshiped Jesus with other believers on Sunday. Some Jewish Christians today still both observe the traditional Sabbath and worship with other Christians on Sunday. Some Christians have used this idea of Sunday as the Sabbath as a religious reason to abstain from work or other activities on this day. While this is certainly reasonable practice, this does not mean the Sabbath day changed to Sunday.

Fifth, many people have questions regarding the application of the Sabbath today. Does the Bible teach that Christians are to abstain from any work on the Sabbath day? Two important biblical passages addressed this matter in the early church.

Acts 15:6–29 is the first passage to address the relationship of the Jewish law with Christianity. The early Christian leaders were divided over whether gentiles (non-Jewish Christians) should have to follow the teachings of the law of Moses, including the observance of the Sabbath. In verses 19–20, they concluded, "We should not trouble those from among the Gentiles who are turning to God, but that we write to them to abstain from things polluted by idols, from sexual immorality, from things strangled, and from blood." Strict observance of the Sabbath was not included.

Romans 14:16 is the second important passage on the topic. In the context of discussing Jewish food laws, Paul wrote, "Do not let your good be spoken of as evil." In other words, in many areas, whether special days or diets, the New Testament allows freedom. If a person feels led to observe the Sabbath on Saturday or even Sunday, they are free to do so. Alternatively, those who treat every day the same (Romans 14:5–6) should be free to do so as well.

However, it is also important to note the biblical emphasis on rest that includes the concept of the Sabbath. Even Jesus observed the Sabbath and often sought to get away for rest. Rest is an important part of our physical and spiritual lives. Without adequate sleep and downtime, we are less effective in our walk with God.

In summary, the Sabbath is not required of Christians today. Instead, it is an option to consider for those who are convicted to do so as well as a pattern reflecting our need to regularly rest to better serve the Lord and share his love with others.

SECTION 8

QUESTIONS ABOUT JESUS

59. WHY IS IT IMPORTANT THAT JESUS WAS BORN OF A
VIRGIN?

One of the key teachings about Jesus is his birth from a
virgin. Why is this teaching so important?

First, the virgin birth is important because it was a
prophecy that confirmed Jesus as the Jewish Messiah.
Isaiah 7:14 teaches, "Therefore the Lord himself shall give
you a sign; Behold, a virgin shall conceive, and bear a son,
and shall call his name Immanuel" (KJV). *Immanuel* means
"God with us." Isaiah wrote these words about seven hundred years before the birth of Jesus.

Second, the virgin birth is a key part of the birth nar-
rative of the New Testament. The angel Gabriel predicted
the virgin birth to Mary:

> Then Mary said to the angel, "How can this be, since I
> do not know a man?"
>
> And the angel answered and said to her, "The
> Holy Spirit will come upon you, and the power of the
> Highest will overshadow you; therefore, also, that
> Holy One who is to be born will be called the Son
> of God. Now indeed, Elizabeth your relative has also
> conceived a son in her old age; and this is now the

sixth month for her who was called barren. For with God nothing will be impossible." (Luke 1:34–37)

Third, God told Joseph in a dream that Mary's child was conceived by the Holy Spirit: "Joseph, son of David, do not be afraid to take to you Mary your wife, for that which is conceived in her is of the Holy Spirit. And she will bring forth a Son, and you shall call His name JESUS, for He will save His people from their sins" (Matthew 1:20–21).

Fourth, the virgin birth means that Jesus was fully human and fully divine. He had a human mother but remained sinless as God the Son. Hebrews 7:26 teaches, "Such a High Priest was fitting for us, who is holy, harmless, undefiled, separate from sinners, and has become higher than the heavens."

Fifth, the virgin birth highlights the eternality or eternal existence of Jesus. His life did not begin in the womb of Mary. Jesus, as the second person of the triune God, has always existed. John 1:1–2 affirms this teaching: "In the beginning was the Word, and the Word was with God, and the Word was God. The same was in the beginning with God" (KJV). Verse 14 also notes Christ's eternal existence: "The Word was made flesh, and dwelt among us, (and we beheld his glory, the glory as of the only begotten of the Father,) full of grace and truth" (KJV). Jesus was not created or made. He is eternal and "became" flesh as part of God's plan to offer redemption and salvation for all people (see 3:16).

In Colossians 1:16, Paul also noted the role of Jesus in the creation of all things: "By Him all things were created that are in heaven and that are on earth, visible and invisible, whether thrones or dominions or principalities or powers. All things were created through Him and for Him." His coming required a virgin birth as Jesus did not need to be conceived. He needed to be birthed from a virgin to fulfill God's prophecies and show himself as God's Messiah.

60. IF JESUS WAS ALREADY PERFECT, HOW COULD HE HAVE "INCREASED IN WISDOM" (LUKE 2:52)?

Luke 2:52 comments on the childhood of Jesus, saying, "Jesus increased in wisdom and stature, and in favor with God and men." Verse 40 adds, "The Child grew and became strong in spirit, filled with wisdom." But how could Jesus increase in wisdom if he is God and is all-knowing?

First, it appears the words are part of the fulfillment of Bible prophecy regarding Jesus as the Messiah. In Isaiah 11:2, written seven centuries earlier, we read, "The Spirit of the LORD shall rest upon Him, the Spirit of wisdom and understanding, the Spirit of counsel and might, the Spirit of knowledge and of the fear of the LORD." Jesus' outstanding wisdom would be one sign that he was the Messiah.

Second, the emphasis is on the human development of Jesus, not his divine nature. In other words, Luke spoke regarding Jesus growing up from infancy into adulthood. As with any person, Jesus would appear to mature physically and in wisdom from the perspective of those around him.

Third, Jesus was all-knowing but also humbled himself regarding the expression of his divine powers. Philippians 2:5–7 teaches, "Have this mind among yourselves, which is yours in Christ Jesus, who, though he was in the form of God, did not count equality with God a thing to be grasped, but emptied himself, by taking the form of a servant, being born in the likeness of men" (ESV). Jesus could not fully reveal his divine powers during his time on earth in order to fulfill God's plan.

Luke 2:52 also concludes the account of Jesus at the temple when he was twelve. His parents had traveled with him to Jerusalem during the Passover and discovered that Jesus was missing during their trip home to Nazareth. After three days, they found him in the temple courts with the religious teachers, holding advanced discussions that amazed those who watched. When his parents asked

Jesus what he was doing, he responded, "Why were you looking for me? Did you not know that I must be in my Father's house?" (v. 49 ESV). The account helps highlight the unique wisdom of Jesus even from a young age. This wisdom was something his mother, Mary, kept in mind (v. 51) as Jesus continued to grow into adulthood.

From a human perspective, Jesus appeared to grow just like any other child. From the Bible's perspective, he was divine and already had perfect wisdom. Despite his divine status, Jesus humbled himself in order to fulfill the plan for God the Father. A close look at this plan reveals his great love for us. Instead of coming the first time as a king, Jesus came as a child and as a servant to offer salvation to all who will believe (John 3:16; Ephesians 2:8–9). As Hebrews 4:15 reveals, "For we do not have a high priest who is unable to sympathize with our weaknesses, but one who in every respect has been tempted as we are, yet without sin" (ESV).

61. WHY DID JESUS COMPARE HIMSELF TO THE BRASS SERPENT OF NUMBERS 21 IN JOHN 3:14–15?

Many people are familiar with John 3:16 but are often confused by the previous two verses: "As Moses lifted up the serpent in the wilderness, so must the Son of Man be lifted up, that whoever believes in him may have eternal life" (John 3:14–15 ESV). Why did Jesus make this comparison?

In Numbers 21:4–9, the Israelites disobeyed the Lord. God sent venomous serpents among the people, causing many of the Israelites to die. The people came to Moses and confessed their sins, asking him to pray to the Lord to remove the serpents. Moses did, and the Lord told Moses, "Make a fiery serpent, and set it on a pole; and it shall be that everyone who is bitten, when he looks at it, shall live" (v. 8). Verse 9 concludes the account, explaining, "Moses made a bronze serpent, and put it on a pole; and so it was, if a serpent had bitten anyone, when he looked at the bronze serpent, he lived."

Hundreds of years later, the bronze serpent appears in Scripture again. Second Kings 18:4 reads, "He removed the high places and broke the sacred pillars, cut down the wooden image and broke in pieces the bronze serpent that Moses had made; for until those days the children of Israel burned incense to it, and called it Nehushtan." King Hezekiah had the pole with the bronze serpent destroyed because many Israelites had turned this powerful symbol into an idol and worshiped it.

Because of the prominence of this bronze serpent in the law of Moses and its role in Israelite history for approximately seven hundred years before the destruction of Jerusalem, its story was likely well-known among the Jewish people living in the time of Jesus. Jesus referred to this bronze serpent as an illustration of rescue or salvation. The Israelites were healed and saved by looking at the bronze serpent on the pole. In a similar way, Jesus would be lifted up on a pole (the cross). Those who look to him will experience eternal life.

This background makes the words of John 3:16 even more powerful: "God so loved the world that He gave His only begotten Son, that whoever believes in Him should not perish but have everlasting life." God did not send his Son to kill the people like the serpents did in Numbers. Instead, Jesus served in a similar manner as the bronze serpent, offering God's healing and restoration in time of need.

The illustration of Jesus being "lifted up" also offers a veiled prediction of Jesus' death on the cross. Just as the bronze serpent was placed upon a wooden pole, Jesus was placed upon a wooden cross to save the lives of those who look to him.

In Galatians 3:13, Paul added another aspect of this comparison with Jesus hanging on the cross: "Christ hath redeemed us from the curse of the law, being made a curse for us: for it is written, Cursed is every one that hangeth on a tree" (KJV). The Jewish law considered anyone who died on a cross as cursed. Jesus took the curse upon himself to offer new life and eternal life to those who believe in him.

62. DOES THE BIBLE TEACH THAT JESUS PREDICTED HIS DEATH?

Christians often talk about Jesus fulfilling prophecy but can be vague regarding examples. When it comes to the death of Jesus, where does the Bible predict how his life would end?

There are two areas to include, both the prophecies of the Old Testament and the predictions by Jesus himself. In the Old Testament, two major predictions about the death of the Messiah are often emphasized. The first is found in Psalm 22. Verses 14–15 speak of the conditions of the Messiah before his death, and verse 16 even hints at the cross: "They pierced My hands and My feet."

The second prediction often emphasized is the suffering servant, or Messiah, in Isaiah 53. Written seven hundred years before the events, Isaiah predicted, "He was wounded for our transgressions, He was bruised for our iniquities; the chastisement for our peace was upon Him, and by His stripes we are healed" (v. 5). Verse 8 adds, "He was taken from prison and from judgment, and who will declare His generation? For He was cut off from the land of the living; for the transgressions of My people He was stricken." Verse 9 also details the burial of Jesus: "They made His grave with the wicked—but with the rich at His death, because He had done no violence, nor was any deceit in His mouth." Jesus died with the wicked, between two criminals. He was then buried "with the rich" in the tomb of Joseph of Arimathea.

In the New Testament, Jesus predicted his death in the Gospels on several occasions. The first time is found in Mark 8:31: "He began to teach them, that the Son of man must suffer many things, and be rejected of the elders, and of the chief priests, and scribes, and be killed, and after three days rise again" (KJV). The prediction is also found in Matthew 16:21 and Luke 9:21–22.

Jesus also predicted his death after the transfiguration: "The Son of man shall be betrayed into the hands of men: And they shall kill him, and the third day he shall be raised again" (Matthew 17:22–23 KJV). This prediction is also noted in Mark 9:30–32 and Luke 9:43–45. The Gospels say that his followers were filled with sorrow when they heard Jesus speak these words (see Matthew 17:23).

Jesus spoke more about his coming death as they traveled for the Passover in Jerusalem shortly before his crucifixion. In Matthew 20:18–19 Jesus said, "Behold, we go up to Jerusalem; and the Son of man shall be betrayed unto the chief priests and unto the scribes, and they shall condemn him to death, and shall deliver him to the Gentiles to mock, and to scourge, and to crucify him: and the third day he shall rise again" (KJV). (See also Mark 9:31; Luke 9:44.)

The Gospels also mention other less specific predictions. For example, Jesus said perfume was used to anoint him for his burial (John 12:7–8) and spoke of going to a place where his followers could not go (John 13:33).

Jesus certainly predicted his death, referring to himself as the fulfillment of the Old Testament's predictions regarding the suffering Messiah. In fact, the Gospels reveal numerous occasions during which he predicted both his death and resurrection to prove himself as the Son of God.

63. How Long Was Jesus on the Cross?

We often hear the account of Jesus dying on the cross, but how long did he remain on it? Was it for only a few minutes, several days, or some other amount of time? The New Testament accounts provide details to help with these questions.

Mark 15:24–25 says, "When they crucified Him, they divided His garments, casting lots for them to determine what every man should take. Now it was the third hour, and they crucified Him." In the Jewish system of time, the third hour was the third hour of daylight, so approximately 9 a.m. This gives us the start time for when Jesus was placed on the cross.

The book of Matthew then adds information about darkness over the land during the time Jesus was on the cross: "Now from the sixth hour until the ninth hour there was darkness over all the land" (27:45). This time period was approximately noon until 3 p.m.

Jesus was taken off the cross and buried before sunset in the tomb of Joseph of Arimathea. Matthew 27:57 says this occurred "when evening had come." Jesus died after about six hours on the cross, from 9 a.m. until 3 p.m., and was taken down shortly afterward and buried before sunset.

The gospel of John also mentions details about the time Jesus was on the cross. He appeared to use the Roman system of time that began counting time at midnight. John 19:14 says that Jesus was sentenced to crucifixion at about the sixth hour: "Now it was the Preparation Day of the Passover, and about the sixth hour." Preparation day was Friday, the day before the Sabbath. This would indicate Jesus was sentenced to crucifixion at around 6 a.m., with his sentence taking place within the three hours following. This is a reasonable amount of time to include walking the distance to the place of the crucifixion and the preparations the soldiers made to place Jesus on the cross.

These details also reveal the chaos that occurred on the night Jesus was betrayed. He would have finished the Last Supper with his followers late Thursday night. They sang a hymn and then walked to the Mount of Olives (Matthew 26:30). Jesus prayed while three of his disciples fell asleep. A mob of people then came and arrested him, and his followers fled. Overnight, Jewish religious leaders examined Jesus in a series of illegal trials to try to sentence him to death. This also involved bringing Jesus before Herod during the early morning hours to have him sentenced to crucifixion.

However, the crucifixion was not the end of the story. Those who followed Jesus mourned the tragic events that led to his death but were soon amazed at the resurrection of Jesus, proven by the empty tomb and his multiple appearances to many people. Jesus then challenged them to take the message to all who would listen, sparking the beginning of the spread of the Christian faith (Matthew 28:18-20; Acts 2:41).

64. WHERE WAS JESUS FOR THE THREE DAYS BETWEEN HIS DEATH AND RESURRECTION?

Jesus died and rose on the third day, but where did he go during the time between his death and resurrection?

Luke 23:43 offers a clear insight regarding where Jesus went after his death. In speaking with the man on the cross who asked Jesus to remember him when Jesus came into his kingdom, Jesus responded, "Assuredly, I say to you, today you will be with Me in Paradise."

Where was paradise? The location was clearly heaven. The only other times the word translated "paradise" is used are in reference to heaven. Paul used the word in 2 Corinthians 12:3-4 when he said, "I know such a man—whether in the body or out of the body I do not know, God knows—how he was caught up into Paradise and heard inexpressible words, which it is not lawful for a man to utter." The other time was in Revelation 2:7, where Jesus said, "To him who overcomes I will give to eat from the tree of life, which is in the midst of the Paradise of God." The tree of life is mentioned again in Revelation 22 (vv. 2 and 14), where the context is the new heavens and earth. It appears clear, based on these passages, that Jesus appeared in the presence of God the Father in heaven between his death and resurrection. John also highlights this answer when Jesus speaks in John 16. In verse 10, Jesus plainly said he was going to "My Father" (see also verses 16 and 17).

In addition to going to heaven, some have suggested that Jesus went into hell as part of his defeat over death. This is based on Ephesians 4:8–10, which refers to Jesus descending into the depths of the earth. This is why the traditional Apostles' Creed includes the phrase that Jesus "descended into hell."

However, the context of the passage contrasts "He also first descended into the lower parts of the earth" (Ephesians 4:9) with Jesus ascending into heaven. The contrast is heaven and earth, not heaven and hell. It is highly unlikely that the apostle Paul intended to communicate that Jesus traveled to hell between the days of his death and resurrection. We do not believe that the text implies that Jesus suffered in the fires of hell; this did not happen and was not how our sins were atoned. Jesus entered into—and returned from—the realm of the dead, but he did not "go to hell" in order to be our Savior.

Some also use 1 Peter 3:18–22 and the sixth verse of Jude to claim that Jesus preached to the spirits from Noah's time during these three days. Why? Because 1 Peter 3:18–20 states, "For Christ also suffered once for sins, the just for the unjust, that He might bring us to God, being put to death in the flesh but made alive by the Spirit, by whom also He went and preached to the spirits in prison, who formerly were disobedient, when once the Divine longsuffering waited in the days of Noah, while the ark was being prepared." However, a better understanding of these passages is that Christ preached through the example and life of Noah in the past. Again, it is highly unlikely that the biblical writers were communicating that Christ was preaching to spirits in hell. Instead, Christ clearly communicated where he would be during the time between his death and resurrection. He was in heaven with the Father, soon returning to earth to prove his role as God's Son through his resurrection from the dead.

65. ON WHICH DAY OF THE WEEK DID JESUS DIE? WHICH DAY WAS HE RESURRECTED?

The traditional teaching of the Bible notes that Jesus was crucified on a Friday and resurrected on Sunday. However, some have suggested that Jesus was crucified on either Wednesday or Thursday. Which view is correct?

The reasons for the controversy regarding this important topic are based on two concerns. Some suggest that Jesus could not have been crucified on Friday based on Matthew 12:40, which predicted Jesus would be like Jonah, who was in the belly of the fish for three days and nights. Others suggest the Last Supper could not have been on Thursday because it did not fit the timeline of the Jewish Passover.

The first argument is the more common of the two. However, Jesus did not predict that he would be in the tomb three days and nights. He said that Jonah served as a sign of his coming death and resurrection. The emphasis was not on a full three days and nights but on his death and resurrection.

Even so, in Jewish culture, even a part of a day counted as a day. Jews also counted their days starting at sunset rather than at sunrise. Jesus was buried on Friday before sunset, marking day one. Mark 15:42 says, "When evening had come, because it was the Preparation Day, that is, the day before the Sabbath," Joseph of Arimathea came and requested the body of Jesus. He placed the body in the tomb that day before sunset. Preparation day was Friday, the day before the Jewish Sabbath on Saturday.

Jesus rose on the third day. We read in 1 Corinthians 15:4 that "he was buried, and that he rose again the third day according to the scriptures" (KJV). The days included part of Friday, all of Saturday, and part of Sunday. We also know Jesus rose on Sunday morning, day three, because all four Gospels refer to the empty tomb on the first day of the week (Matthew 28:1; Mark 16:2; Luke 24:1; John 20:1). Sunday was the first day of the week in the Jewish calendar. Jesus' crucifixion on Friday and resurrection on Sunday do not contradict Matthew 12:40.

But what about the second concern related to the timing of the Last Supper? Some have argued that Jesus and his followers would not have eaten the Passover meal on Thursday night. However, Passover extended over a full week. Many families gathered for special meals together multiple times throughout the holiday period of eight days in addition to the special celebration on the Passover Day. If the crucifixion happened on Friday as we believe, it seems most logical that Jesus would have shared the "upper room" Passover meal with his disciples on Thursday night.

Jesus was crucified on the Passover Day in an amazing fulfillment of Bible prophecy, confirming him as the Messiah and the Lamb of God, who alone takes away the sins of the world, offering eternal life to all who believe. Even the centurion who stood by the cross who saw how Jesus died stated, "Truly this Man was the Son of God!" (Mark 15:39).

66. HOW DO WE KNOW JESUS WAS RESURRECTED?

Unlike today, in biblical times there was no ability to broadcast live video of the resurrection of Jesus or his exiting the tomb. Instead, people used the evidence of eyewitnesses to prove matters in a court of law and for other important areas of life. The evidence for the resurrection is based on the testimonies of more than five hundred people who said they saw Jesus alive again, including in multiple locations over a forty-day period.

First Corinthians 15:5–8 offers a list of many of the eyewitnesses of the resurrected Jesus. Paul wrote, "He was seen by Cephas, then by the twelve. After that He was seen by over five hundred brethren at once, of whom the greater part remain to the present, but some have fallen asleep. After that He was seen by James, then by all the apostles. Then last of all He was seen by me also, as by one born out of due time." Paul noted that most of these eyewitnesses were still alive over twenty years after the resurrection when he wrote his letter. The claim offered a strong basis of evidence that the readers would have otherwise easily dismissed.

The list of eyewitnesses also includes both people friendly and unfriendly to the resurrection. In other words, those who followed Jesus might be tempted to make up the story, but those who did not believe he was the Messiah would not have done so. The fact that James, the half brother of Jesus who doubted him, was among those who saw Jesus alive again shows the diversity of eyewitnesses.

In addition to hundreds of eyewitnesses, the empty tomb of Jesus provides strong proof of his resurrection. The Jewish religious leaders claimed Jesus' disciples had stolen the body (Matthew 28:11–15). However, tradition holds that ten of the original disciples were killed for their faith (excluding John) without a single one of them claiming he had stolen the body. In addition, no one ever found Jesus' body. Still today, you can travel to Jerusalem and visit the empty tomb of Jesus. His bones are not there. Why not? He is alive. He also offered evidence of being alive in a variety of other ways. Many people saw and heard him. Others touched him (Luke 24:39). He ate food (Luke 24:41–43).

Many also argue that we can know Jesus is alive by the growth of the Christian faith and the lives Jesus has changed. He has certainly transformed our world in major ways. In the AD 20s, there was no church. A century later, churches existed across the Roman Empire and beyond. By the fourth century, Christianity was the empire's official religion. Today, more than two billion people adhere to the Christian faith.

On a personal level, we can also experience the many ways Jesus has changed our own lives and the lives of those around us. What is the best explanation for the many lines of evidence regarding the eyewitness accounts, empty tomb, spread of Christianity, and changed lives? The most reasonable explanation is that the message is true. Jesus is alive, proving himself as God's Son, the Savior of the world.

67. WHO SAW JESUS AFTER HIS RESURRECTION?

The New Testament records that more than five hundred different people saw Jesus alive after his resurrection. A close look offers substantial evidence of the many individuals who experienced the resurrected Lord.

Jesus first appeared to Mary Magdalene at the empty tomb on Sunday morning. The account in John 20:11–18 says, "Jesus said to her, 'Mary!' She turned and said to Him, 'Rabboni!' (which is to say, Teacher)" (v. 16).

The second appearance was to the other women who saw Jesus near the empty tomb on Sunday morning. In addition to Mary Magdalene, Matthew 28:8–10 includes the other Mary along with others. Luke 24:10 specifically names Joanna, Mary the mother of James (likely the same as the other Mary in Matthew), and unnamed other women.

Jesus also appeared to the following:

- The two men on the road to Emmaus on Sunday afternoon. They included one man named Cleopas and another unnamed man (Luke 24:13–32).
- Peter on Sunday (Luke 24:33–35; 1 Corinthians 15:5)
- The apostles, excluding Thomas (John 20:19–25)
- The apostles with Thomas a week later (John 20:26–29)
- Seven of the apostles at the Sea of Galilee (John 21:1–13). The group included "Simon Peter, Thomas called the Twin, Nathanael of Cana in Galilee, the sons of Zebedee, and two others of His disciples" (v. 2). The sons of Zebedee were James and John.
- Five hundred people at once (1 Corinthians 15:6)
- James, his half brother (1 Corinthians 15:7)
- The eleven disciples before ascending to heaven (Matthew 28:16–20; Luke 24:50–53; Acts 1). Some interpret these appearances as happening at two different events though they likely refer to the same occasion.

After his ascension, Jesus also appeared to Stephen before his death (Acts 7:55–56), to Paul (recorded in Acts 9:3–6 and also in 1 Corinthians 15:8–9), and to the apostle John in Revelation 1:9–19. However, these three appearances were likely visionary or in some way uniquely different from Christ's physical resurrection appearances.

Not including the people who saw Jesus in a vision after his ascension, at least 513 different people appear to have seen the risen Lord. This is far more than enough evidence to seriously consider the claim that Jesus literally rose from the dead.

SECTION 9

QUESTIONS ABOUT SALVATION

68. WERE PEOPLE BAPTIZED IN THE OLD TESTAMENT?

The New Testament practice of baptism was not common during the Old Testament, but similar practices of cleansing and washing were. The law of Moses required cleansing or washing in a variety of situations, foreshadowing the cleansing that baptism would provide. Baptism first took place during the ministry of John the Baptist, and later those who believed in Jesus were also baptized.

In the cultural period in which John the Baptist and Jesus lived, some Jewish groups practiced daily washings or baptisms. John the Baptist utilized this culturally known concept in a one-time washing during his ministry at the Jordan River. It appears that he called people to repentance, with individuals responding by faith and immersing themselves in the water in response to his teaching (Matthew 3).

John's outreach affected the lives of many people in Israel. Mark 1:5 states, "All the land of Judea, and those from Jerusalem, went out to him and were all baptized by him in the Jordan River, confessing their sins." Those baptized included tax collectors, who were often considered traitors to the Jewish people (Luke 3:12).

In Matthew 3:13, Jesus came to John the Baptist for his own baptism: "Jesus came from Galilee to John at the Jordan to be baptized by him." John sought to stop him, claiming John himself should be baptized by Jesus. Jesus urged John to baptize him to "fulfill all righteousness" (3:15) as part of the beginning of his public ministry.

Jesus and his disciples continued this practice of baptism. John 4:1–3 records, "When the Lord knew that the Pharisees had heard that Jesus made and baptized more disciples than John (though Jesus Himself did not baptize, but His disciples), He left Judea and departed again to Galilee." Jesus apparently did not baptize anyone, but his followers did so when people responded to his teaching.

When Jesus prepared to ascend to heaven after his resurrection appearances, he told his followers to continue the practice of baptizing those who believed in him: "Jesus came and spoke to them, saying, 'All authority has been given to Me in heaven and on earth. Go therefore and make disciples of all the nations, baptizing them in the name of the Father and of the Son and of the Holy Spirit'" (Matthew 28:18–19).

Still today, believers in Christ are called to be baptized as a step of obedience in following the Lord. Those who followed God in the Old Testament followed the law of Moses. Today, believers follow the teachings of Jesus, showing their commitment to him through baptism as a public profession of faith.

69. WHAT IS BAPTISM, AND WHY IS IT IMPORTANT?

Baptism is the English translation of the Greek word *baptismos*, which means "to wash or dip." The practice involved a person going into water to demonstrate their desire for cleansing from sin and their commitment to live for God.

While baptism does not provide salvation, it is a command Jesus gave in the New Testament for those who follow him.

Baptism has been an important part of the church since before its beginning. John the Baptist preached about the coming Messiah and baptized in the Jordan River those people who believed his message and repented.

Jesus provided an example for believers through being baptized (Matthew 3:13-17). His followers baptized people who believed in Jesus and his teachings during his earthly ministry (John 4:1-3).

Before Jesus ascended to heaven, he commanded his followers to baptize believers: "Jesus came and spoke to them, saying, 'All authority has been given to Me in heaven and on earth. Go therefore and make disciples of all the nations, baptizing them in the name of the Father and of the Son and of the Holy Spirit'" (Matthew 28:18-19). When the church began on the day of Pentecost in Acts 2, the apostles baptized more than three thousand people who believed that day. "Those who gladly received his word were baptized; and that day about three thousand souls were added to them" (Acts 2:41). The practice extended to other believers outside of Jerusalem. In 8:12, "Both men and women were baptized." A man from Ethiopia was also baptized by Philip after believing in Jesus (v. 38). Saul, also known as the apostle Paul, was baptized after he believed in Jesus (9:10-18).

Gentiles (non-Jews) who believed in Jesus were baptized (10:47), including those Paul led to faith in Christ during his mission trips. Sometimes entire households were baptized, as was the case when Lydia's family believed (16:15) and the Philippian jailer and his family (16:33). Many have used these passages to argue for infant baptism, though these accounts do not specifically mention infants.

Baptism was traditionally designated for a person who believed in Jesus. It was also originally by immersion, as John the Baptist's ministry at the Jordan River suggests. The practice of baptism throughout the history of the church is one of just two sacraments stated in the Bible and practiced universally in churches (the other is communion, also called the Eucharist or Lord's Supper). Jesus commanded that every believer is to be baptized to identify with the example of Jesus and to follow in obedience to his command.

Though baptism does not provide salvation, the practice is a key teaching in the New Testament that pertains to all followers of Jesus. Those who have believed in Jesus and have not yet been baptized since coming to faith should consider doing so as soon as possible.

70. HOW DO YOU TALK WITH SOMEONE WHO BELIEVES HELL DOES NOT EXIST BECAUSE GOD IS LOVE?

How can we more effectively communicate the important biblical concept of a real, literal hell? People often ask us how to talk about hell with someone who does not believe it exists. For example, Eastern religions like Buddhism and Hinduism teach that a person reincarnates into another life form after death. Even many people who believe in God do not believe in hell.

Establishing a common foundation is the key way to begin. If a person claims to believe in the teachings of the Bible, then we can use those passages to show that the existence of heaven and hell is undeniable. The Bible, including Jesus himself, makes many references to hell. In Matthew alone, Jesus discusses hell seven times (5:22, 29, 30; 10:28; 18:9; 23:15, 33). The New Testament also mentions hell in Mark and Luke, as well as in James 3:6 and 2 Peter 2:4. The Old Testament directly mentions hell more than a dozen times, ranging from Deuteronomy to Habakkuk.

For a person who does not believe in the teachings of the Bible, a different approach is necessary. The definitive word on what happens after death should come from one who has actually been into the realm of the dead...and come back again. And Jesus has done this. Only Christ's words are unequivocally trustworthy on matters of eternity because only Jesus has power over the grave. And Jesus taught that hell is real (Luke 16:19–31) and that he has power to send people there if they reject him (Matthew 10:28).

And so, for those who reject this and say otherwise, we must ask, "Jesus taught and warned us that hell is real. Was he right, or was he wrong?" No mortal has the authority to pronounce that Jesus was incorrect on something (Has the skeptic walked on water? Raised the dead?). So we'll accept the testimony of the only one who ever did these things...Jesus.

Additionally, all cultures, interestingly, have two narratives somewhere in their folklore: some type of creation story and some idea of a final judgment. The concept of reward for the just and punishment for the unjust is deeply embedded in the human psyche. It seems reasonable that since essentially all major cultures in history have held to a concept of ultimate judgment, there is an element of truth in this belief. But we say that there is more than an element of reality here: hell has the support of reason, written revelation, and the teachings of Christ.

Scripture is clear that a person lives once and then a judgment occurs: "As it is appointed unto men once to die, but after this the judgment" (Hebrews 9:27 KJV). We do not come back as another life form. We only live once here on earth, but we live forever in eternity. Jesus offered a clear example in Luke 16:19–31. He told an account of Lazarus and a rich man. Lazarus died and went to "Abraham's bosom," or side, indicating he was in heaven with the Lord. The rich man died and was in "Hades," or hell. This passage in Luke describes hell as a place of torment that includes flames (vv. 23–24). It is also unchanging and eternal, with no ability to move from hell to heaven: "Between us and you there is a great gulf fixed, so that those who want to pass from here to you cannot, nor can those from there pass to us" (v. 26).

In addition to only living once and the eternality of hell, Scripture also clearly teaches that God is love and desires for people to spend eternity with him in heaven. First John 4:8 directly states, "God is love," and many other biblical passages also articulate the teaching. John 3:16 states that "God so loved the world that He gave His only begotten Son."

God is a judge; it is part of his nature. What does a judge do? He renders an opinion, based on whether a person upholds or breaks the laws. Because the human race has frequently—some would say *zealously*—broken the laws of God, he must administer judgment.

God is also acting as a judge when he accepts the sacrifice of Jesus for the acquittal of sinners who, as a result, go to heaven. If we wrest from God, the judge, the authority to send some to hell, then to be consistent, we are also removing from him the right to shower grace in admitting others to heaven.

We've found that many people want to deny that hell exists because they have a loved one who passed away without knowing the Lord. While this is a difficult situation, we cannot deny a clear biblical teaching simply because of the emotional effect it has on us. Instead, we can acknowledge that God is a perfect judge who will rightly determine the eternity of any person, including our loved ones when we are uncertain whether they knew the Lord.

The reality of hell is also important to remember as we seek to share Christ with others. We do not know when our own life or the lives of others will end. We are called to boldly proclaim the Lord with all who will listen so that more people may join us in heaven for all eternity.

71. HOW CAN I KNOW IF I AM TRULY SAVED?

How can a person know if he or she is truly saved? The Bible does not leave us in doubt but offers specific information to help us know for certain whether we truly know the Lord.

Salvation is by faith in Jesus Christ. Romans 10:9–10 teaches, "If you confess with your mouth the Lord Jesus and believe in your heart that God has raised Him from the dead, you will be saved. For with the heart one believes unto righteousness, and with the mouth confession is made unto salvation." The first question to ask yourself is whether you have believed in Jesus as God's Son who rose from the dead.

Second, a person who is saved will also admit to being a sinner. First John 1:8 says, "If we say that we have no sin, we deceive ourselves, and the truth is not in us."

Third, do you follow the teachings of the Lord? Any person can say they believe in Jesus, but obedience is the evidence of true faith. This obedience does not save us but shows that we are saved. First John 2:3–6 says, "Now by this we know that we know Him, if we keep His commandments. He who says, 'I know Him,' and does not keep His commandments, is a liar, and the truth is not in him. But whoever keeps His word, truly the love of God is perfected in him. By this we know that we are in Him. He who says he abides in Him ought himself also to walk just as He walked."

Fourth, do you love other followers of Jesus? A true believer will be known for his or her love for other Christians. First John 3:14–15 says, "We know that we have passed from death to life, because we love the brethren. He who does not love his brother abides in death. Whoever hates his brother is a murderer, and you know that no murderer has eternal life abiding in him."

It is common for a person to have doubts about their faith in the Lord, especially during their earlier years of living for God. However, 1 John 5:13 is clear that we do not have to remain in doubt: "These things I have written to you who believe in the name of the Son of God, that you may know that you have eternal life, and that you may continue to believe in the name of the Son of God." Many times, the doubts that we have regarding our faith come from one of two sources. Sometimes we question our salvation because we have slipped into a time of sin. Instead of doubting our faith, 1 John 1:9 challenges us to confess our sin and restore fellowship with God: "If we confess our sins, He is faithful and just to forgive us our sins and to cleanse us from all unrighteousness."

The second cause of doubt is when we rely on our emotions. Emotions are good, but they can also deceive us into believing things that are not true. Instead of depending on your emotions when it comes to your salvation, let the truths of Scripture remind you how to come to Christ. One important way to do this is to reflect on your own personal testimony. Whether writing it down, telling your story to someone else, or simply thinking back to when you first believed, this reflection can refuel your heart in serving the Lord. Like David in Psalm 51:12, look to God to "restore to me the joy of Your salvation, and uphold me by Your generous Spirit."

We don't have to guess if we have eternal life. We can know and have confidence that we will experience heaven with the Lord through our faith in Jesus, admitting our sin, growing in obedience, and loving other believers.

72. CAN A PERSON LOSE THEIR SALVATION?

Is it possible for someone who has been saved to later lose his or her salvation? Many Bible-believing Christians have struggled with this issue, but we believe Scripture leaves no doubt. If a person truly received eternal life, God will not take this gift away.

First, salvation is a gift. We cannot earn it, so there is no reason to believe that God would take back something he has freely shared. Ephesians 2:8–9 is clear regarding salvation: "By grace you have been saved through faith, and that not of yourselves; it is the gift of God, not of works, lest anyone should boast."

Second, God changes the believer into a new creation. In 2 Corinthians 5:17 we read, "Therefore, if anyone is in Christ, he is a new creation; old things have passed away; behold, all things have become new."

Third, the promise of eternal life begins when we come to faith in Jesus. Many do not realize that when we are saved, our eternal life has already started. John 3:16 promises, "God so loved the world that He gave His only begotten Son, that whoever believes in Him should not perish but have everlasting life."

Fourth, verses 24–25 of Jude give us God's guarantee that the Lord will keep us from stumbling: "Now to Him who is able to keep you from stumbling, and to present you faultless before the presence of His glory with exceeding joy, to God our Savior, who alone is wise, be glory and majesty, dominion and power, both now and forever. Amen."

But what about those verses that seem to teach that a person can lose their faith? The most common passage people use to prove that Christians can lose their salvation is Hebrews 6:4–6: "It is impossible for those who were once enlightened, and have tasted the heavenly gift, and have become partakers of the Holy Spirit, and have tasted the good word of God and the powers of the age to come, if they fall away, to renew them again to repentance, since they crucify again for themselves the Son of God, and put Him to an open shame." However, we can also understand this passage as referring to people who have seen God at work and have turned down the gift of eternal life. If a person can see the salvation of other people, experience

God's Spirit at work around them, and see God's Word in action and still reject salvation by "falling away," there is no other means to motivate them.

Additionally, verses 9–11 indicate that the author of Hebrews emphasized the assurance of salvation for his believing readers: "Beloved, we are confident of better things concerning you, yes, things that accompany salvation, though we speak in this manner. For God is not unjust to forget your work and labor of love which you have shown toward His name, in that you have ministered to the saints, and do minister. And we desire that each one of you show the same diligence to the full assurance of hope until the end."

To summarize, salvation is a gift that God gives to those who believe. He will not take his gift back but instead makes us a new creation, promises to keep us until we are before him in heaven, and has already started eternal life in us. Those unclear passages that seem to indicate that we can lose our salvation are referring to those who have never truly believed. The Lord will bring to him all those who have truly believed.

73. Do infants and young children go to heaven when they die?

One of the most difficult experiences in life is for a parent to lose a young child. In addition to the physical loss of the baby or child, Christian parents are also concerned about what happens to the child's soul. Does the Bible teach that those who are too young to believe go to heaven?

Some believe that the Bible is not clear on the issue, but we argue that it is. The most direct passage on the matter is found in 2 Samuel 12:22–23. David's infant son passed away after David fasted and prayed for God to spare him. When he discovered the news of his child's passing, David cleaned himself, worshiped the Lord, and ate again. His servants found the actions odd and asked David why he had responded this way. King David replied, "While the child was alive, I fasted and wept; for I said, 'Who can tell whether the LORD will be gracious to me, that the child may live?' But now he is dead; why should I fast? Can I bring him back again? I shall go to him, but he shall not return to me."

We can understand the phrase "I shall go to him" in a general sense, indicating that both David and his infant child would go to the grave together. However, interpreting the passage in this way would not explain why David felt comforted over his child's loss. Instead, he clearly believed that his child had died and that he would see him again. Where would David see his son again? In heaven. This understanding also fits the love of God for children. Even Jesus was known for his heart for young people. "Let the little children come to Me, and do not forbid them; for of such is the kingdom of God," he said (Mark 10:14; Luke 18:16).

Scripture clearly indicates the Lord's love for children in other places in both the Old and New Testaments as well. God is a perfect judge. He will clearly determine eternity in the perfect way for all people, including young children who pass away, children who die in the womb or in a stillbirth, as well as those with limited intellectual abilities.

Sometimes Christians speak of an age of accountability, suggesting there is a certain time at which a person is old enough to either believe or reject the gospel. However, the Bible does not give an exact age. Samuel worshiped the Lord when he was very young (1 Samuel 2:18), and others come to the Lord later in life. Instead of expecting a child to decide to receive Jesus at an exact age, it is important to teach our children about salvation and encourage them to believe as God prepares their heart at just the right moment.

Trusting in God's will does not mean that we should neglect ministering to children and students, especially if you are a parent. Parents hold the primary responsibility to share the gospel with their own children, encouraging them to believe as they understand their sinful nature, their need for God, and the salvation Jesus provides. Many people begin their faith in Jesus as children, and our goal as the church should be to encourage and strengthen these young believers to hold firm to biblical truths throughout their lives.

74. HOW SHOULD WE RESPOND TO THOSE WHO SAY THERE IS MORE THAN ONE WAY TO HEAVEN OR THAT EVERYONE GOES TO HEAVEN?

Over the past generation, one false teaching that has become popular in our culture is the belief that there is more than one way to heaven. Some even believe that everyone, or at least almost everyone, goes to heaven. How should we respond to those with this perspective?

First, we must affirm that we only know heaven exists because God's Word has revealed it. If the Bible is the source of our knowledge regarding heaven, it should also be our source for how to reach heaven.

Second, a close look at the Bible's teachings regarding heaven explain that there is only one way to enter. Acts 4:12 includes the message of Jesus taught to the apostles: "Neither is there salvation in any other: for there is none other name under heaven given among men, whereby we must be saved" (KJV). In John 14:6, Jesus said, "I am the way, the truth, and the life. No one comes to the Father except through Me." That's very clear, coming directly from Jesus. In 11:25, Jesus added, "I am the resurrection and the life. He who believes in Me, though he may die, he shall live."

Third, we cannot let difficult situations distract from the Bible's clear teachings regarding salvation. For example, those who argue that everyone goes to heaven immediately turn to questions about those who have never heard about Jesus or ask about what happens to infants who die before they are old enough to believe in Jesus. These are important questions, but they do not change Scripture's core message regarding how lost people become saved.

Fourth, address the question behind the question. In other words, many people wish to believe there is more than one way to go to heaven because of friends or family members who follow other religions or beliefs. Don't be afraid to challenge why a person holds a position. Questioning can often lead to a discovery of the real concerns a person has that you need to address.

Fifth, you can also ask the other person to define what they mean when they say they believe there is more than one way to heaven. Answers commonly include some form of earning a way to heaven. This type of response may allow you to address salvation as a free gift of faith.

Scripture teaches there is only one way to heaven—faith in Jesus Christ. Ephesians 2:8–9 offers a clear path: "By grace you have been saved through faith, and that not of yourselves; it is the gift of God, not of works, lest anyone should boast."

Don't be afraid to confront a person's misconceptions about heaven. This is an important step in the process of sharing Christ with others and helping them to know the Lord. Through your prayer, compassion, and genuine discussion, God can work through you to help others know the one true God and his way of salvation.

75. CAN A CHRISTIAN'S NAME BE ERASED FROM THE BOOK OF LIFE?

Revelation mentions a Book of Life where the names of believers are written. Can a person's name be erased from this Book of Life?

Let's first look at where the Bible's final book shares this information. Revelation mentions a Book of Life on seven occasions. From the start, John recorded the words of Jesus that indicate believers will not have their names erased. In Revelation 3:5, John wrote, "He who overcomes shall be clothed in white garments, and I will not blot out his name from the Book of Life; but I will confess his name before My Father and before His angels."

There is also a second mention of the Book of Life found in 13:8: "All who dwell on the earth will worship him, whose names have not been written in the Book of Life of the Lamb slain from the foundation of the world." The verse explains that unbelievers will worship the Antichrist but also issues a sobering warning related to this discussion.

What is that sobering warning? It is that those not named in the Book of Life will fall for the strong delusion (see 2 Thessalonians 2:11), will worship the Antichrist, and will be irremovably separated from God. The solution? As soon as you are aware of the reality of the gospel, turn your heart to Christ, which will result in your name being recorded in his book.

Revelation 17:8 also refers to unbelievers as not being named in the Book of Life: "Those who dwell on the earth will marvel, whose names are not written in the Book of Life from the foundation of the world, when they see the beast that was, and is not, and yet is." Notice that the verse teaches that the names of believers have been written in the Book of Life "from the foundation of the world." This powerful truth informs us that every person who has or will ever believe in the Lord is already known by him and has been written in his book. He will not erase a person's name, as he has prepared from eternity past for those who know him.

Revelation 20:15 states, "Anyone not found written in the Book of Life was cast into the lake of fire." This verse indicates judgment through eternal separation from the Lord for those not in this book.

Revelation 21:27 says, "There shall by no means enter it anything that defiles, or causes an abomination or a lie, but only those who are written in the Lamb's Book of Life." Everyone in the new heaven and earth will be named in the Book of Life.

Revelation 22:19 adds, "If anyone takes away from the words of the book of this prophecy, God shall take away his part from the Book of Life, from the holy city, and from the things which are written in this book." This reference indicates both a Book of Life and states God will "take away his part" from those who take away from Revelation. This warning seems to be toward unbelievers who seek to criticize God's words.

In addition to Revelation, Philippians 4:3 says Clement and other Christians Paul mentioned have their name in the Book of Life: "I urge you also, true companion, help these women who labored with me in the gospel, with Clement also, and the rest of my fellow workers, whose names are in the Book of Life." This should encourage us to know our names are written in his book as believers. It should also challenge us to treat other believers well, knowing we share together in this wonderful gift of being known by the Lord and that we have eternity ahead of us.

SECTION 10

QUESTIONS ABOUT MARRIAGE AND PARENTING

76. WHAT DOES THE BIBLE SAY ABOUT THE IMPORTANCE OF FAMILY?

The word *family*, the concept of family, and references to family units appear over one hundred times in the Bible, more than prayer or even heaven. Family is paramount to God. He proves it in the very first book of the Bible and the very first chapter. Here, we see family in the Godhead, the Trinity, appearing in verse 26: "Then God said, 'Let us make man in our image, after our likeness'" (ESV).[6]

When God called Abraham out of Haran, he called him and his family (Genesis 12:4–5). The importance of family appears in the Mosaic covenant. Two of the Ten Commandments deal with the cohesiveness of the family. The fifth commandment about honoring parents preserves the authority of parents in family matters, and the seventh prohibiting adultery protects the sanctity of marriage. Many stipulations in the Mosaic law protected marriage and the family. The importance of the family was so vital to God that he codified it in his national covenants with Israel and with us.

6 For more information on the Trinity, read "25. What is the Trinity?"

Why is family so important to God? Family pays all the dividends. It makes us who we are and establishes the foundation of who we will become. Invest in the woman, man, or children God has given you, and you will win in other areas. But lose family or marriage, and you will lose in many areas. Nothing will be more lasting or more rewarding than family. The stock market will rise and fall. Your career will have successes and failures. Prioritize family, and God will bless your other endeavors. "Seek first the kingdom of God and his righteousness, and all these things will be added to you" (Matthew 6:33 ESV).

We've spoken at thousands of churches and probably prayed with hundreds of individuals and couples over the years. No one has regretted that they'd spent too much time with their families. Many wish they'd spent more time with their family, been more involved, held each other more, and said "I love you" more.

Where you focus your time and energy reveals the things you value most in life. Is it the relationships—time and memories with family and friends? The things that seem to consume most of our time—hours in the office, hobbies, diversions—will all dissolve one day. Indeed, you can't take it with you. Work and other necessities require attention and time, more at certain stages of life than others. We're not diminishing making a living, paying the bills, and fulfilling obligations. While we must fulfill those obligations, we must also deliberately choose to invest time, money, and devotion into our families. Careers, trophy collections, or mortgages have a place but cannot replace what can be lost by not investing time, effort, and love in our families. What will you be left with when all the other stuff is gone? We pray it's family.

If you need to lower your standard of living to raise your quality of family life, do it! Solomon, one of the wealthiest men of all time, wrote, "Do not toil to acquire wealth...When your eyes light on it, it is gone, for suddenly it sprouts wings" (Proverbs 23:4-5 ESV). Many successful and famous people grew up in abject poverty, but they succeeded in life because their parents invested what they did have—time and love. You have no greater treasure to guard or more valuable heritage to preserve than your family.

Family problems are nothing new, and the Bible doesn't gloss over them. Even families that prioritize God have problems because we're human. Eli, Samuel, David, and others had wayward children, broken homes, or relationships damaged by sin. The first spouses caved to the serpent's temptation. Adam blamed his wife and God: "The woman whom you gave to be with me, she gave me fruit of the tree, and I ate" (Genesis 3:12 ESV). Only a few chapters later, Cain and Abel's sibling rivalry turned deadly. In a fallen world, those we should love the most—our families—can become the ones we fight with the most. It takes work, but that can change, just as it did for Jacob and Esau, who hated each other in Genesis 27 but forgave and reunited in chapter 33. We see the beauty and intimacy God intended for marriage in the Song of Solomon. Still, we see jealousy among wives— one negative consequence of polygamy—in the stories of Hannah, Leah, and Rachel. In Luke 15, Jesus told the parable of a prodigal son who treated his father with contempt, but it is also the story of a loving father who never gave up on his son. Even when family is imperfect, God gives us hope that it can be restored and relationships healed.

The Bible clearly explains how family members should treat each other: Husbands should love their wives as Christ loves his church (Ephesians 5:25, 33). Wives should respect their husbands and submit to their leadership (1 Peter 3:1). Children should obey their parents and honor them (Ephesians 6:1-4; Exodus 20:12). The key to family harmony is submission, a concept that goes against our human nature. Ephesians 5:21 says to "submit to one another out of reverence for Christ" (NIV). We all defend our rights, champion our causes, and assert our agendas over others. Selfishness is natural, but it is destructive for a family. When we submit to the needs and wishes of others, we are most like Christ, who submitted to God the Father not because it was best for him or because it would make him famous, rich, happy, or satisfied. Jesus is our model because he submitted to God's will for our best.

Most family problems could be reduced or eliminated if we followed the instructions in Philippians 2:3–4: "Do nothing from selfish ambition or conceit, but in humility count others more significant than yourselves. Let each of you look not only to his own interests, but also to the interests of others" (ESV). That spirit of humility and treating others as Jesus would treat them can resolve many of our family and relationship problems.

The concept of family is extremely important in the Bible, both in a physical and a theological sense. God's plan for creation was for men and women to marry and have children. The Bible focuses on family to show us how to prioritize and live in familial relationships for our good. Marriage and family are the essential building blocks of human society. Protect them and invest in their success like your life and your future depend on it. They do.

77. WHAT DOES IT MEAN TO BE A GODLY PARENT?

Parenting may be the most frustrating and exhausting work in the world. At the same time, it can be the most rewarding and fulfilling. Whether you are a happily married couple, a blended family, or a single parent, you can be a godly parent with God's help. You couldn't have a better example or child-raising partner. The Bible is a great resource for challenging times and a guidebook for parenting, raising godly children, and building a protective hedge around your family. Our highest priority in godly parenting is teaching our children the truth of God's Word. If God is an expert parent, and he is, we can follow his parenting advice, which is in his Word.

When you raise strong children, you are creating the future of that safe and thriving society. A strong family and stable home are more than a wholesome place to live and build relationships. The family unit is the underpinning of a successful and civil society. It all begins at home with godly parenting. What is godly parenting from a biblical perspective? Let's start by examining God's view of family and parenting.

Someone wisely said, "More is caught than taught." This principle is nowhere truer than in parenting. Children learn more by observation than by instruction. God understood this. Jesus said, "Follow me" over twenty-five times. The apostle Paul said, "Be imitators of me, as I am of Christ" (1 Corinthians 11:1 ESV). He urged the Philippians to "join in imitating me, and keep your eyes on those who walk according to the example you have seen in us" (Philippians 3:17 ESV). Your example will outlast your words; what example will your children remember?

Your relationship with God should be accessible and casual for your child to see and hear. Teaching God's words and ways should be a natural flow of life that your children don't have to be told because they observe it all the time in action. This only happens if God's Word is part of your life. Read it. Live it. Apply it. "These words that I command you today shall be on your heart. You shall teach them diligently to your children, and shall talk of them when you sit in your house, and when you walk by the way, and when you lie down, and when you rise" (Deuteronomy 6:6–7 ESV). Moses is simply saying to make your talk about God match your lifestyle.

Godly parents give their children an example to live up to. You are sowing seeds into their little spirits with every word, seeds that will grow and produce fruit. What fruit do you want to see in your child? Tell a child he is stupid enough times and he will believe you. When he fails in school, he won't be surprised because he thinks he is stupid. If you tell a child she will be incredibly successful because of how smart she is, that seed will also grow and blossom. She will have high expectations for herself and strive to prove how right you are.

Discipline is part of godly parenting. Godly discipline is balanced, loving, and imposed properly; it builds a child's sense of worth and value. Proverbs 13:24 uses strong language on this, saying that discipline demonstrates love and that parents who refuse to discipline hate their child. Proverbs 19:18 says, "Discipline your children, for in that there is hope; do not be a willing party to their death" (NIV). Respect, courage, and a sense of pride come from balanced, consistent discipline.

Discipline and correction are often unpleasant in the moment, but discipline must never cross the line into abuse. Hebrews 12:11 says, "For the moment all discipline seems painful rather than pleasant, but later it yields the peaceful fruit of righteousness to those who have been trained by it" (ESV). We should accompany all discipline with loving instruction and encouragement for the child to do better next time.

Finally, involve your children in a healthy family environment at church, where they will see your same values, discipline, and love reflected in other godly parents. This helps them to see that such behavior should be the norm. Let your children see you studying the Bible and read it with them. A children's Bible is a great gift. Imagine the seeds you sow if your child learns to read by reading the Bible!

Children are a heritage from the Lord. Invest in them. Love them. Sow seeds of a godly life in them and nurture those seeds with consistent discipline and examples. You will see those seeds blossom and grow when you demonstrate a godly life before them.

78. WHAT DOES IT MEAN THAT GOD IS A FATHER TO THE FATHERLESS?

God could have chosen any language of affiliation with us: Commander, Magistrate, Ruler. But with humans, God chose the language of relationship—family. Psalm 68:5 says, "Father of the fatherless and a defender of widows is God in his holy habitation" (ESV).

God presents himself as a father because we all know what a father is and does. Even those with earthly fathers who failed them still have an intrinsic understanding of what a good father *should* be. God planted that understanding in our hearts. We all share the same need to be loved, valued, protected, and cherished for who we are. Ideally, our earthly father should fill that role, but if he doesn't, God promises he will.

Jesus enjoyed this unique fatherly relationship and promised it to us. He instructed his followers to address God as "Father," teaching them to pray, "Our Father in heaven, hallowed be Your name" (Luke 11:2). God said, "I will be a father to you, and you shall be sons and daughters to me, says the Lord Almighty" (2 Corinthians 6:18 ESV).

God's attributes can reflect both a father and mother. Isaiah 66:13 says, "As one whom his mother comforts, so I will comfort you" (ESV). Although God represents the love of either parent, he uses masculine language to denote strength, protection, and provision. That does not mean mothers do not demonstrate those character traits, for many do. But in the time and culture when the Bible was written, those were primarily associated with fathers.

Parents love their children; most would give their lives for them, but God's love exceeds even the most caring parent. His love is inexhaustible, completely unselfish, and eternal. Just like a parent's love, we can't do anything to earn God's love, and we cannot do anything to lose it. Romans 8:39 confirms, "Neither height nor depth, nor anything else in all creation, will be able to separate us from the love of God that is in Christ Jesus our Lord" (NIV).

God has a special place in his heart for widows, orphans, and the fatherless. In first-century times, to be an orphan was nearly a death sentence. People in pagan cultures enslaved, abused, and even sacrificed orphans to their deities. Orphans were disposable but not to God. He demonstrated his love for all of us by showing his love for those considered the least of society—the fatherless. Psalm 27:10 says, "For my father and mother have forsaken me, but the LORD will take me in" (ESV).

It is an unfortunate reality and national tragedy of our time that many children grow up in fatherless homes. The US Census Bureau in 2020 reported, "Children living with a mother only is the second most common U.S. living arrangement, a number that has doubled since 1968. About 7.6 million (11%) children lived with their mother only in 1968 compared to 15.3 million (21%) in 2020."[7] The tragedy of father-absent homes contributes to many issues later in life; from something as fundamental as confidence and self-worth to keeping kids off drugs and out of prison, fathers serve a God-appointed purpose in the home.

While single moms and single dads do admirable work under incredibly difficult circumstances, the ideal home is still God's model of one man and one woman living in love and devotion to each other for life. As this has become less and less the norm, society reflects the ills and

---

7   Paul Hemez and Chanell Washington, "Number of Children Living Only with Their Mothers Has Doubled in Past 50 Years," United States Census Bureau, April 12, 2021, https://www.census.gov/library/stories/2021/04/number-of-children-living-only-with-their-mothers-has-doubled-in-past-50-years.html.

imbalance that grow out of rejecting God's ideal pattern for family and for society as a whole.

Fatherlessness is not a new problem; that's why the Bible addresses it. What is God's solution? The ideal solution is that men would follow God's plan and remain a godly example in the home: stay, work, love their wives, display compassion and love for their children, and teach kids to play, work, and conquer. When a father is absent or even when he is physically present but emotionally unapproachable, God promises to be a father to the fatherless.

That is not merely a throwaway promise or a lovely poetic phrase. How is God a father to the fatherless? He promises to protect: "Leave your fatherless children; I will keep them alive, and let your widows trust in me" (Jeremiah 49:11 ESV).

God promises never to leave: "The LORD himself goes before you and will be with you; he will never leave you nor forsake you. Do not be afraid; do not be discouraged" (Deuteronomy 31:8 NIV). Some fatherless children feel like throwaways. Jesus promised, "All that the Father gives me will come to me, and whoever comes to me I will never cast out" (John 6:37 ESV). The fatherless can cry out to him when they are in trouble: "Call upon me in the day of trouble; I will deliver you, and you shall glorify me" (Psalm 50:15 ESV).

Above all, God's love compels him to act. If your child has a need, you meet it. Your children don't have to beg you for food or medical attention. But for even the most loving parent, there are limits to what we can do for our children. God's love and parental devotion are not limited. He demonstrated that in his ultimate act of love for all humanity: "For God so loved the world, that he gave his only Son, that whoever believes in him should not perish but have eternal life" (John 3:16 ESV).

79. What Does the Bible Say About Sex Before Marriage?

God's design for sexual intimacy was originally created to be enjoyed within the context of marriage between one biological male and one biological female. Genesis 2:24 teaches, "A man shall leave his father and mother and be joined to his wife, and they shall become one flesh."

Believers who choose to have sex before marriage will experience shame or guilt. As verse 25 shares, "They were both naked, the man and his wife, and were not ashamed." Even with modern birth control methods, there is no medical invention to remove the guilt associated with a believer who has sex before marriage. God can forgive and restore, but his forgiveness does not give us the right to bypass his teachings for our own pleasures.

Those who do not follow the Lord may disregard this biblical teaching, but those who seek to obey the teachings of Scripture will hold strong to the Bible's standard of waiting for sexual intimacy until marriage and reserve sex for within the marriage. In 1 Corinthians 5:10 Paul wrote, "I wrote to you in my epistle not to keep company with sexually immoral people. Yet I certainly did not mean with the sexually immoral people of this world, or with the covetous, or extortioners, or idolaters, since then you would need to go out of the world." The apostle noted that believers are called to a higher standard of holy living. We can't expect to avoid associating with unbelievers who sin, but we are called to oppose the practice of believers living in sexual sin, including premarital sexual activity.

In addition to disobeying God's teachings regarding sexual purity and the guilt associated with sex before marriage, there are other concerns to consider. Unexpected pregnancy or sexually transmitted diseases remain common in such relationships, despite well-intended efforts at protection. What begins as a one-time pleasure may result in a lifetime of complications. Another consideration is that it takes away from the gift of sexual intimacy to be shared with a future spouse. Many believers have entered marriage with the shame of past sexual activity that has impacted their marriage for years.

These factors are also important to consider when planning for marriage. Though it is increasingly common in Western cultures to wait longer to get married, this delay can lead to more temptations before marriage. In 1 Corinthians 7:8–9 Scripture teaches, "I say to the unmarried and to the widows: It is good for them if they remain even as I am; but if they cannot exercise self-control, let them marry. For it is better to marry than to burn with passion." It may be appropriate to consider marriage somewhat earlier in certain cases to help avoid this issue.

Scripture is clear that God created sex, and he created it to be shared as a gift between a husband and wife within marriage. Speaking of adultery, Proverbs 6:27 says, "Can a man take fire in his bosom, and his clothes not be burned?" (KJV). Those who act outside of God's commands will reap consequences associated with choosing to fall to temptation.

80. HOW ARE CHILDREN A BLESSING FROM THE LORD?

Solomon's Psalm 127 is a Psalm of Ascent. It was one of a series of psalms pilgrims would recite as they walked up the long road to the Temple in Jerusalem. Families would recite it together as they walked hand in hand up the steep hill. Psalm 127:3 says, "Behold, children are a heritage from the LORD, the fruit of the womb a reward" (ESV). Some translations say children are a gift or an inheritance. Using this term, Solomon affirms the ancient Near East belief that children are God's gift to parents.

Children are a great joy and pleasure, as demonstrated by Proverbs 23:24: "The father of the righteous will greatly rejoice; he who fathers a wise son will be glad in him" (ESV). It can be equally heartbreaking when a son or daughter disobeys or rebels bringing heartache to their parents.

The Bible places immense value on families and encourages parents to have children and enjoy raising them. No one would deny that having a family involves enormous responsibility, expense, and time demands, yet there is also no denying the immense rewards. Solomon focuses on the joys of a large family when he adds, "Like arrows in the hand of a warrior are the children of one's youth. Blessed is the man who fills his quiver with them!" (Psalm 127:4–5 ESV).

Parents bear the huge responsibility of child-rearing and all that entails. God commanded us to teach children his ways, to encourage them to follow him, and to honor and glorify God and serve him throughout their lives. "Train up a child in the way he should go; even when he is old he will not depart from it," Proverbs 22:6 (ESV) tells us. This verse is as much a promise from God as it is a challenge to parents. God will do his part and keep his promise. We must do ours.

The Bible also identifies children as a blessing from the Lord because children demonstrate unique character traits God desires in his kingdom followers.

Children are humble and unassuming. Jesus said, "Truly, I say to you, unless you turn and become like children, you will never enter the kingdom of heaven. Whoever humbles himself like this child is the greatest in the kingdom of heaven" (Matthew 18:3–4 ESV).

Children are unafraid. Jesus loved children, and they weren't afraid to approach him. Children have an intuitive way of knowing which adults like them and want them around and which ones do not. When the children surrounded Jesus, some adults sent them away. "When Jesus saw it, he was indignant and said to them, 'Let the children come to me; do not hinder them, for to such belongs the kingdom of God. Truly, I say to you, whoever does not receive the kingdom of God like a child shall not enter it'" (Mark 10:14–15 ESV). Jesus loves children.

Children are unimpressed by rank or status. When the disciples were disputing who among them was the favorite or had the most authority, Jesus rebuked them by saying, "Not so with you. Rather, let the greatest among you become as the youngest, and the leader as one who serves" (Luke 22:26 ESV).

Children need nourishment. This statement may seem oddly out of place in a chapter about what the Bible says about parenting and children. Everyone knows a child needs food. But the Bible makes a singular and revealing point about children and uses that point to admonish adults to follow the innocent and unassuming ways of a child: "Like newborn infants, long for the pure spiritual milk, that by it you may grow up into salvation" (1 Peter 2:2 ESV). When a child is hungry, nothing will stand in their way. We need that same drive, intention, and sense of urgency to follow God and find him in his Word, the Bible. Nothing can replace nourishment. Not knowledge, experience, happiness, or money; nothing feeds your stomach like food. Equally, nothing feeds our spirit—the part of us most like God—like being filled with his Word.

God uses children and family to bring joy and blessing—a gift—that nothing else provides. Children are a heritage, a blessing, and a gift from God. When they seem like an inconvenience or at their most annoying moment, look at your child and tell them, "You are a gift from God to me! I love you like Jesus."

81. WHAT DOES THE BIBLE SAY ABOUT CHILD ABUSE?

The Bible does not specifically use the term *child abuse*. God holds a special place in his heart for children. While the Bible endorses discipline, instruction, and correction for children, it never supports abuse of any kind. As the creator and sustainer of the earth and its inhabitants, God knows the importance of giving birth to the next generation and helping them grow up into healthy, strong adults.

No one demonstrated God's attitude toward children more than Jesus. When the disciples tried to keep children from coming to Jesus, he rebuked them and welcomed the children. Mark 10:16 tells us, "He took the children in his arms, placed his hands on them, and blessed them" (NIV). We can imagine Jesus sitting and talking to each child and blessing them individually. Imagine a line of kids waiting to speak to Santa. That is likely an accurate image of the scene. From the size of the crowd, there were likely hundreds of children, yet every one of them crawled up on Jesus' lap. He held and blessed each one.

God knows children are the key to continuing a prosperous and thriving society; they are our future, and our very survival depends on their mental and emotional health. He commands us to instruct them, love them, nurture them, and "bring them up in the discipline and instruction of the Lord" (Ephesians 6:4 ESV).

Abuse defies and damages every principle of godly parenting. Instead of showing love, abuse reveals anger and hate. Instead of showing that someone is in control, it indicates loss of control and rebellion. Instead of correcting, it only punishes, more akin to revenge than correction or discipline. Rage, spite, loss of control, and lashing out in physical abuse are exactly the opposite of the actions you want your child to mimic. Godly discipline is not abusive.

The Bible warns against ungodly and uncontrolled anger. "'In your anger do not sin': Do not let the sun go down while you are still angry, and do not give the devil a foothold" (Ephesians 4:26–27 NIV). Proverbs 29:22 adds, "A man of wrath stirs up strife, and one given to anger causes many transgressions" (ESV). Raging anger is a sin and should be confessed to God before dealing with a child. Too often, anger leads to abuse when parents vent their frustrations on a child. If you don't have control of yourself, you will teach your child to lash out when they are angry too.

Most abuse originates in rage, sin, or power or results from parents who were abused when they were young. The cycle often repeats. If the abused adult who never fully recovered abuses their child, they perpetuate the same behavior to another generation. In 2021, researchers released a study on the intergenerational transmission of child maltreatment in *Lancet Public Health*. Over thirty-eight thousand people participated, with data collected from 1986 to 2017. To date, it is the largest, most exhaustive study on inherited or multigenerational abuse ever conducted. They reported a substantial correlation between a mother who suffered maltreatment in childhood and the likelihood of her child experiencing maltreatment. The study details, "Children of mothers with a history of both substantiated maltreatment and out-of-home care had 6.3 times the risk of any CPS [child protection system] involvement, 13.7 times the risk of substantiated maltreatment, and 25.8 times the risk of having time in out-of-home care, compared with children of mothers with no CPS involvement."[8] Sadly, they concluded what the Bible had warned

---

8   Jason M. Armfield et al., "Intergenerational Transmission of Child Maltreatment in South Australia, 1986–2017: A Retrospective Cohort Study," *Lancet Public Health* 6, no. 7 (April 2021): 457, https://doi.org/10.1016/S2468-2667(21)00024-4.

all along: Sin begets (gives birth to) more sin. Abuse repro-duces more abuse.

If you were abused, is that the legacy you want to pass on? If you were abused, your children don't have to grow up that way. Give your pain and guilt and emotional hurt to Jesus. He is able and willing to take it. Let go of the anger, resentment, and hate. Let go of that weight of abuse so you don't dump it on your children and increase the possibility they will do the same and dump it on the next generation. Jesus said, "Come to me, all you who are weary and burdened, and I will give you rest" (Matthew 11:28 NIV). You can end the cycle.

Abusers of children mistreat them in several ways, all of which God abhors. The Bible clearly condemns sexual abuse, warning against sexual sin repeatedly (1 Corinthians 6:9, 18; Galatians 5:19–20; Jude 1:7; Matthew 5:28; Hebrews 13:4). Sexual abuse violates a person physically, emotion-ally, and spiritually. It destroys their self-image, damages their self-respect, and scars their understanding of God's divine order for sex in love and marriage. When sexual boundaries are broken, it destabilizes a child's concept of appropriate love, caring hugs, and physical touch, making them vulnerable to more abuse.

The Bible also prohibits psychological and emotional abuse. Ephesians 6:4 explains that improper discipline provokes a child and overshadows any constructive train-ing: "Fathers, do not provoke your children to anger, but bring them up in the discipline and instruction of the Lord" (ESV). Harsh, unloving verbal abuse, emotional manipula-tion, or volatile outbursts create an unstable environment. There is never a time for belittling, name-calling, constant fault-finding, or telling a child they can't do anything right. Hurtful words wound as much as physical abuse and are often more enduring. Proverbs 12:18 says, "There is one whose rash words are like sword thrusts, but the tongue of the wise brings healing" (ESV). Psalm 57:4 warns that our words can be like the teeth of a wild animal that tear apart.

Proverbs 4:22 promises that a father's words stay in a child's heart: "[Good words] are life to those who find them and health to one's whole body" (NIV). The "whole body" means mind, body, and soul. Godly words heal and build up. Abusive words hurt, tear down, and criticize. We should follow Ephesians 4:15–19, which says, "Rather, speaking the truth in love, we are to grow up in every way into him who is the head, into Christ, from whom the whole body, joined and held together by every joint with which it is equipped, when each part is working properly, makes the body grow so that it builds itself up in love" (ESV). Words can build up or tear down. Use healing words, never destructive words.

If you are a loving, caring parent who has never experienced abuse, continue that tradition with your children. If you are one of the many who experienced abuse as a child, you choose how to raise your children. Don't repeat the mistakes and hurts. Be a loving, gentle, balanced parent who disciplines in love. Speak with love and compassion. Demonstrate Jesus to your children; they will honor you and follow Jesus because they see the same love and compassion in him.

82. WHAT SHOULD OUR TOP PRIORITIES BE IN FAMILY LIFE?

The Bible does not lay out a step-by-step order for family relationships. However, it does say that our top priority never changes: "Love the LORD your God with all your heart, with all your soul, and with all your strength" (Deuteronomy 6:5). When you commit your heart and soul and strength to loving God, you make him the first priority. Make him the center of your family through your words and deeds, involving every family member in church and attending regularly. Don't send your kids to church; take them with you. Hebrews 10:25 says, "Not neglecting to meet together, as is the habit of some, but encouraging one another, and all the more as you see the Day drawing near" (ESV).

God is first; if you are married, your spouse comes next. Ephesians 5:25 tells men, "Husbands, love your wives, as Christ loved the church and gave himself up for her" (ESV). Christ's first priority—after obeying the Father—was the church. He set an example for all husbands: God first, then his wife. A married man is to love his wife as Christ loved the church. Wives prioritize in the same way: God first, then their relationship with their husband, committing to him "as to the Lord" (Ephesians 5:22 ESV).

Since husbands and wives are second only to God in priority and because Ephesians tells us that a husband and wife are "one flesh" (Ephesians 5:31), it stands to reason that the result of the marriage relationship—children—should be the next priority. Parents must prioritize raising godly children who will be the next generation and repeat that investment in their families. If they see mom and dad loving unconditionally, caring for others above themselves, and demonstrating loving devotion to each other, they are more likely to do the same. Proverbs 22:6 says, "Train up a child in the way he should go; even when he is old he will not depart from it" (ESV).

Beyond our immediate family, we ought to honor our parents. Deuteronomy 5:16 tells us to "Honor your father and your mother...so that you may live long and that it may go well with you" (NIV). It does not specify an age limit, which means we should honor them as long as our parents are alive. Once we reach adulthood, we are no longer commanded to obey them; we must obey God for ourselves, but honor has no expiration date. After everyone else comes the rest of the extended family. First Timothy 5:8 says, "If anyone does not provide for his relatives, and especially for members of his household, he has denied the faith and is worse than an unbeliever" (ESV).

Because believers are a family in God, we also owe fellow Christians some priority. Romans 14 tells us not to look down on our brothers or sisters or do anything that would make them stumble. In both Corinthian letters, Paul instructed the church on how to live in harmony, love each other, serve each other, and demonstrate a godly life. Later, Paul told a church, "Serve one another humbly in love" (Galatians 5:13 NIV). He gives similar advice to another church: "Be kind and compassionate to one another, forgiving each other, just as in Christ God forgave you" (Ephesians 4:32 NIV).

Our priorities are God, spouse, children, parents, extended family, brothers and sisters in Christ, and the rest of the world. Occasionally, one requires immediate attention out of this order, but the long-term priorities remain the same. We never forget we owe the message of salvation to the whole world. Matthew 28:19 reminds us that God's priority is all the world, not just us or our families. We must never forget to "go therefore and make disciples of all nations" (ESV).

83. WHAT IS THE BIBLICAL PERSPECTIVE ON DOMESTIC VIOLENCE?

Narrowly defined, *domestic violence* is an act or threatened act of violence against someone with whom the perpetrator is or has previously been in an intimate relationship. Domestic violence often brings to mind a battered wife or child abuse. Watching or hearing one parent abuse the other can have severe psychological implications, even if the children are not physically harmed.

Domestic violence is often about power and control or the loss of them. While violence has physical connotations, domestic violence or abuse can also be nonphysical.

Some abusers manipulate victims emotionally or financially. Verbal and sexual abuse are other forms of domestic violence. Domestic violence can impact men and women of all ages, socioeconomic classes, education levels, or religions. Like child abuse, those who suffered abuse or witnessed abuse as a child are likelier to abuse someone in a cycle of violence.

Domestic violence and abuse sharply contrast with God's plan for families. Genesis 1 and 2 depict two people becoming one: helping, serving, loving, and working together toward a common goal. Paul and Peter explained our duty to our spouses. Paul said emphatically that a husband's body is not his own but is subject to his loving wife. In turn, she, in love and devotion, yields to him, but neither does so because of fear. "For the wife does not have authority over her own body, but the husband does. Likewise the husband does not have authority over his own body, but the wife does" (1 Corinthians 7:4 ESV). This is not ownership-like control. This type of ownership resembles how you would appreciate and pamper an inherited antique china doll or a restored classic car handed down from a great-grandparent. It is a cherished responsibility, not a dominating control and definitely not abuse.

Marriage is the most perfect reflection of God's love for us, demonstrated by how a husband would give his life for his wife. Jesus died for us, and his ultimate sacrifice illustrates how much God loves us and how far he will go to save and protect us. Domestic violence destroys God's divine order for marriage and forces one partner to live in terror. Jesus did not manipulate. He told his disciples, "Whoever wants to become great among you must be your servant...just as the Son of Man did not come to be served, but to serve, and to give his life as a ransom for many" (Matthew 20:26–28 NIV).

If you or someone you know is in an abusive relationship, get help. No one deserves to suffer from abuse. In the US, the National Domestic Violence Hotline offers information and resources at 800-799-SAFE (7233) or online at www.thehotline.org.

QUESTIONS ABOUT CHURCH AND CHRISTIAN LIVING

84. WHAT DOES THE BIBLE SAY ABOUT TATTOOS?

One popular question we have received over the years is whether the Bible allows Christians to get a tattoo. The practice of tattoos has become so common in our society that it feels like everyone has at least one. As followers of Christ, we should certainly consider what Scripture says before doing something that could impact our bodies for the rest of our lives.

The most common reference in the Bible to tattoos is found in Leviticus 19:28: "You shall not make any cuttings in your flesh for the dead, nor tattoo any marks on you: I am the LORD." During the time of Moses, tattoos were common, but they were also associated with those who followed other gods. The law condemned the Jewish people from getting tattoos so that they would be distinct from the ungodly cultures around them.

Today's Christians, however, are free from the Jewish law and look to the teachings of the New Testament for guidance. In 1 Corinthians 6:19–20, Paul wrote words about sexual activity in a passage that could also apply to tattoos: "Do you not know that your body is the temple of the Holy Spirit who is in you, whom you have from God, and you are not your own? For you were bought at a price; therefore glorify God in your body and in your spirit, which are God's." Anyone considering a tattoo should ask whether the particular choice of design would honor the Lord. While a small cross or similar tattoo might be honorable to God, many other choices would not.

A related passage is found in 10:23–24: "All things are lawful for me, but not all things are helpful; all things are lawful for me, but not all things edify." Some translations end this sentence with the word *expedient* or *beneficial*. In other words, a believer is free in Christ but, at the same time, is responsible for the welfare of other members of the family of believers. Paul ended verse 24 with these words: "Let no one seek his own, but each one the other's well-being." We are to consider the possible implications of a decision we make, especially if that choice is basically irreversible.

In addition, there are practical issues to consider. Will a particular tattoo make current or future employment difficult? Are there any personal health issues to consider? Is it a wise financial decision? How would this particular tattoo affect relationships with family or those you are trying to reach for the Lord?

Children should also honor their parents in this area. While living at home under a parent's authority, a child should refrain if a parent instructs against a tattoo (see Ephesians 6:1–3).

Some have even argued that Christians should get tattoos by claiming Jesus will have one when he returns. Why? Revelation 19:16 says, "He has on His robe and on His thigh a name written: KING OF KINGS AND LORD OF LORDS." While this might refer to a marking directly on the leg of Jesus, it could also refer to a covering on his leg. In either case, Jesus won't be "inked up" in his glorified body, so we should not equate this reference with modern tattoos.

Before getting a tattoo, each person should be completely certain it is the right personal choice. Romans 14:16 says, "Do not let your good be spoken of as evil." God may lead one person to do something yet lead another person to refrain. So long as a person is seeking the Lord's will in this matter, we should allow freedom rather than judgment regarding the choice of a tattoo.

85. WHAT DOES THE BIBLE TEACH ABOUT FEMALE PASTORS?

The New Testament notes two different categories of church leaders. They included elders (also referred to as bishops or pastors) and deacons. A look at the characteristics and qualifications of these two groups of leaders provides the best response to the question of whether women can serve as pastors.

The qualifications for elders or pastors are provided in both 1 Timothy 3 and Titus 1. In 1 Timothy 3:1, we read, "If a man desires the position of a bishop, he desires a good work." Some translations have rendered "a man" to "anyone," but a natural reading of the text refers to males. In addition, verse 2 notes the bishop or elder/pastor must be the husband of one wife, certainly referring to men. Verse 5 adds more male-specific details: "If a man does not know how to rule his own house, how will he take care of the church of God?" The pronouns throughout verses 1 through 7 are also male. In Titus 1, we find the same pattern. The pastor or elder is noted as a "man" in verse 6. He must also be the husband of one wife and have faithful children. These verses also use male pronouns.

Further supporting male pastors is the observation that all elders who are named in the New Testament church are male. Females played critical roles in the early church but not as elders.

The evidence is clear that the New Testament teaches that only men are qualified to serve as a pastor or elder, but does this extend to today? This is where we find the most controversy. In many cases, the concern is with the title given to a person leading in a church. For example, the difference between a children's pastor and children's director is sometimes only one word, but a gifted woman can certainly serve in leading children in the church.

Some have included 1 Timothy 2:12 in the discussion and the controversial words, "I do not permit a woman to teach or to have authority over a man, but to be in silence." It appears Paul had to address women who disrupted worship services at times, but we are not to understand the word *silence* as never speaking or never being involved in a church service. The emphasis here is to be quiet during worship gatherings rather than to seek to stand out or take over worship services. It was not and is not a ban on women ever speaking when people are gathered for worship.

While some churches or denominations may offer more opportunities for women to lead than others, it is clear that a woman did not serve as an elder in the New Testament. In today's churches, this applies, at the very least, to the senior pastor or teaching pastor role in the local church. Women serve in many vital leadership roles in today's churches, but we must also seek to reflect an accurate application of Scripture to church leadership.

We also encourage you to talk with your own church leadership regarding any concerns in this area. The Bible says the local church should be a place for growth and maturity among believers. There should be room for genuine discussion and opportunities for women to flourish in ministry leadership without going beyond the teachings of Scripture.

86. WHAT IS FASTING, AND SHOULD CHRISTIANS FAST TODAY?

Traditionally, fasting is going a period of time without food in order to focus on the Lord. In the Old Testament, the law required fasting on the Day of Atonement each year, a practice many Jews continue today. Fasting was also part of mourning and repentance, with Moses, Elijah, and Jesus each fasting for an amazing forty-day period! Does Scripture command Christians to fast, or should they at least consider doing so today?

In the Old Testament, several people fasted in addition to Moses and Elijah. In Judges 20:26, the Israelites fasted as part of a time of mourning. In 2 Samuel 12:16 and 21, David fasted and prayed for God to spare his infant child from death. Queen Esther fasted for three days without food or drink to seek God's protection for the Jewish people. She also called others to join her: "Go, gather all the Jews who are present in Shushan, and fast for me; neither eat nor drink for three days, night or day. My maids and I will fast likewise" (Esther 4:16). Those who buried Saul and his sons also fasted for seven days (1 Samuel 31:13). We could add other examples, but these show that the Jews included fasting during times of prayer, during mourning, and for spiritual times set apart to worship the Lord.

The New Testament does not require that Christians fast, but it does assume many will. When Jesus spoke about fasting in Matthew 6:16–17, he said, "When you fast," referring to the times the Jews who originally heard his teachings fasted. Early Christians followed the example of Jesus in fasting. For example, in Acts 13:2–3, early church leaders in Antioch fasted and prayed before sending Paul and Barnabas on their first missionary journey.

Paul and Barnabas fasted and prayed before they later selected church elders in cities where churches had started through their missionary work: "When they had ordained them elders in every church, and had prayed with fasting, they commended them to the Lord, on whom they believed" (Acts 14:23 KJV).

In 1 Corinthians 7:5, Paul mentioned married couples sometimes fasting and praying: "Do not deprive one another except with consent for a time, that you may give yourselves to fasting and prayer." Paul personally fasted on many occasions (2 Corinthians 6:5; 11:27).

Why would we consider fasting today? For the same reasons past followers of God chose to do so. Sometimes, we fast as part of mourning over the loss of a loved one. At other times, we may go without food for a period of time to focus on a special prayer need. Sometimes we may simply fast to draw closer to the Lord. James 4:8 says, "Draw near to God and He will draw near to you."

For those of us who live in a culture in which we have many food choices, choosing to abstain from food, whether for a meal, a day, or more, can allow God to work in our lives in a special way as we draw near to him. However, we must also use much care in making any major change to our diet. Even going one day without food may require other changes in our schedule, and consulting a doctor is important for those with health issues or anyone considering a longer fast.

87. WHAT DOES THE BIBLE SAY ABOUT THE BAPTISM OF INFANTS?

The baptism of infants has long been a point of controversy, both between Catholic and some Protestant churches as well as among various Protestant denominations. What does the Bible say about infant baptism?

A look at baptism in the Bible reveals two clear traits. First, people were baptized after they made a commitment to believe in Jesus as Lord. On the day of Pentecost in Acts 2, those who believed were baptized, with three thousand people added to the church that day (v. 41). Christians followed this pattern throughout the book of Acts and in the New Testament. Young people were certainly baptized as well but only after believing in Jesus.

A second important aspect regarding baptism in the New Testament is that there is no clear example of an infant being baptized. Many have interpreted passages to reach this conclusion. For example, 1 Corinthians 7:14 is referred to as an example: "For the unbelieving husband is sanctified by the wife, and the unbelieving wife is sanctified by the husband: else were your children unclean; but now are they holy" (KJV). The verse, however, is not discussing baptism. It is indicating that when a parent (or the head of the home) becomes a follower of Christ, the odds go up dramatically that other members of the family will as well.

Others have used the household of Cornelius (Acts 10:47–48), the household of Lydia (Acts 16:15), the family of the Philippian jailer (Acts 16:32–33), and similar examples as "proof" of infant baptism since baptisms appeared to include the entire family. While these examples may seem to favor infant baptism, no infants are mentioned. It is only an assumption that infants were included.

In Middle Eastern cultures and many parts of the world today, when the leader of a household believes and is baptized, other members are as well. Why? Because families usually make decisions in community. Though salvation is a personal decision, communal societies often wait until the family leader chooses to believe before the family makes a public commitment to baptism.

Two other examples also offer evidence of those who are intended for baptism. First, John the Baptist was the person who popularized baptism ahead of Christ's ministry in the New Testament. He baptized men and women in the Jordan River as they believed in his message of the coming Messiah and confessed their sins. Scripture records no examples of infant baptism by John.

The second example is found in the Great Commission. As Jesus prepared to ascend to heaven, he told his followers, "Go therefore and make disciples of all the nations, baptizing them in the name of the Father and of the Son and of the Holy Spirit" (Matthew 28:19). Baptism was associated with faith in Christ, not with infants.

Those who argue in favor of infant baptism generally use the comparison of the practice with that of circumcision among the Jews in the Old Testament. A child is "set apart" through infant baptism and joins in covenant as part of a believing family. Regardless of the long historical practice of infant baptism that began during the early centuries of church history, the tradition is not based on the examples found in the New Testament.

While we do not seek to condemn families who choose to baptize their infant children, we do not advocate for it. There is no need to perform the ritual. Instead, parents are called to raise their children to believe in Christ and to be baptized at the appropriate time as a public expression of their faith.

88. WHAT IS THE BIBLICAL VIEW OF SUICIDE? DOES A BELIEVER WHO COMMITS SUICIDE GO TO HEAVEN?

Suicide occurs when a person dies due to inflicting wounds on himself or herself. The Bible condemns murder, with many people including suicide in this category. Many people misunderstand the tragedy of suicide, and Christians should take the utmost care to understand what Scripture says regarding the topic and learn how to help themselves or others who have suicidal thoughts.

First, the Bible is clear that even godly people can have suicidal thoughts. For example, the prophet Jonah said he was angry enough to die after God held back from judging the people of Nineveh (Jonah 4:8). We may be tempted in this area but should never act on the impulse to end our own life.

Second, evidence is increasingly clear that suicide is not something a person does under normal circumstances. In other words, people once spoke of suicide as a person "killing themselves." Today, counselors and others generally use the wording "death by suicide." Those who die by suicide are often suffering from depression, strong grief, the influence of addictive substances, or mental health issues that may cause someone to make decisions they might not otherwise.

Third, those close to a person who has died by suicide often struggle with guilt, believing it was their fault. This is not the case. You may feel bad over the loss of a loved one who died by suicide, but you were not the one who ended the person's life. We may mourn over the loss of a loved one whose life ends by suicide, but we should not take responsibility for it.

Fourth, it is essential to understand the Bible's view about the eternal destiny of those who die from suicide. There has long been a misconception that suicide is some type of unforgivable sin that automatically sends a person to hell. This is certainly not the case. A person who dies by suicide will experience eternity like every other person. Those who have believed in the Lord Jesus Christ will have eternal life (John 3:16), but those who die apart from Christ will spend eternity apart from him.

There are many other misconceptions related to suicide and Scripture. For example, some have argued that Samson chose suicide by dying with the Philistines. This false picture of his life is contradicted by Judges 16:30, in which Samson said, "Let me die with the Philistines!" He did not die by suicide. Samson sacrificed himself to defeat the enemies of God's people during a time of war.

Perhaps the most tragic example of suicide in the Bible is the example of Judas Iscariot, the disciple who betrayed Jesus for thirty silver coins. He denied Jesus and died by suicide. His actions ended his earthly life and left him eternally separated from God. This judgment was not due to his suicide. It was due to his lack of belief in who Jesus really was. Jesus said, "The Son of Man indeed goes just as it is written of Him, but woe to that man by whom the Son of Man is betrayed! It would have been good for that man if he had not been born" (Matthew 26:24).

Those who die by suicide do not automatically go to hell. Instead, each person must determine their faith in Jesus Christ. Suicide is a tragic action that ends life early. We should encourage those who have thoughts regarding suicide to seek help immediately. In the US, if you or someone you know is struggling with suicidal thoughts, please call 988 or visit 988lifeline.org to reach the 988 Suicide & Crisis Lifeline.

89. Why is communion (the Eucharist or Last Supper) important for Christians?

Jesus left two important rituals for Christians to follow. The first one, baptism, is a one-time act that a believer undertakes after choosing to believe in Jesus. The second one, communion, is an ongoing practice that believers share. Both actions remember the death and resurrection of the Lord, with communion proclaiming the Lord's death until his return.

The apostle Paul provided details about this practice to the Corinthian Christians:

> I received from the Lord that which I also delivered to you: that the Lord Jesus on the same night in which He was betrayed took bread; and when He had given thanks, He broke it and said, "Take, eat; this is My body which is broken for you; do this in remembrance of

Me." In the same manner He also took the cup after supper, saying, "This cup is the new covenant in My blood. This do, as often as you drink it, in remembrance of Me." For as often as you eat this bread and drink this cup, you proclaim the Lord's death till He comes. (1 Corinthians 11:23–26)

Paul referred to communion in three ways in this passage: a remembrance, a covenant, and a proclamation. Communion is a remembrance because the practice leads believers to think about the broken body and spilled blood of Jesus on the cross as a sacrifice for sins.

Communion is also a covenant. A covenant is an agreement between two or more groups or people. In this context, the covenant is an agreement between the Lord and believers, part of the new covenant or promise by God to offer salvation through Jesus. It was a fulfillment of Jeremiah 31:31, a new covenant with the house of Israel and Judah. Matthew 26:28, Mark 14:24, and Luke 22:20 also emphasize communion as part of the new covenant with believers. Paul also noted this new covenant in 2 Corinthians 3:6, where he called himself a minister of the new covenant. Hebrews reveals the new covenant as making the old covenant obsolete (Hebrews 8:7–13; 9:15), calling Jesus the "Mediator of the new covenant" (12:24).

Communion is also a proclamation. The practice informs and instructs those who participate. In the Old Testament, the Jews annually remembered God's rescue from Egypt through the Passover. They placed blood from a slaughtered lamb at the top and sides of the doorways while each family ate roasted lamb together with unleavened bread inside the home.

Jesus provided the new covenant that offers communion as a similar practice for Christians to remember his death as the Lamb of God who takes away the sins of the world. When we take the bread and drink from the cup, we proclaim or teach the way of salvation through Jesus Christ (Acts 4:12).

Both baptism and communion also remind us of the need for a community of believers. We can read Scripture or pray individually, but we cannot truly experience baptism or communion alone. We are called to join together with other Christians as family, enjoying the relationships with one another and with the Lord as we remember and proclaim his death, resurrection, and future return: "Let us consider one another in order to stir up love and good works, not forsaking the assembling of ourselves together, as is the manner of some, but exhorting one another, and so much the more as you see the Day approaching" (Hebrews 10:24–25).

90. WHAT DOES THE BIBLE TEACH ABOUT CHRISTIANS AND TITHING?

The word *tithe* means "tenth" and is first found in Genesis 14:20. Abraham gave the priest Melchizedek a tenth or tithe of all the spoils from war against the enemies who captured his nephew Lot and his family.

The Jewish law formalized the practice of the tithe into a requirement for the people of God (Leviticus 27:30). The tenth was not the only offering but was the foundation of several gifts and offerings that the Jews were to bring to the Lord. The Lord at times condemned the Israelites through his prophets for not obeying the law to bring the tithe to the Lord. Malachi 3:8–10 is perhaps the best-known example:

> "Will a man rob God?
> Yet you have robbed Me!
> But you say,
> 'In what way have we robbed You?'
> In tithes and offerings.
> You are cursed with a curse,

for you have robbed Me,
even this whole nation.
Bring all the tithes into the storehouse,
that there may be food in My house,
and try Me now in this,"
says the LORD of hosts,
"If I will not open for you the windows of heaven
and pour out for you such blessing
that there will not be room enough to receive it."

In the New Testament, Jesus taught that we are not to give so that others would see but that we are to do so in quiet (Matthew 6:1–4). Jesus warned the Pharisees that they should have given a tenth of their resources while also not neglecting justice, mercy, and faithfulness (Matthew 23:23). The first Christians were Jews who likely followed the Jewish practice of giving the tithe while also giving to meet the needs of early believers. Acts 2:44–45 describes giving in the early church: "All who believed were together, and had all things in common, and sold their possessions and goods, and divided them among all, as anyone had need."

In 1 Corinthians 16:1–2, Paul advised the Corinthians Christians about giving: "Concerning the collection for the saints, as I have given orders to the churches of Galatia, so you must do also: On the first day of the week let each one of you lay something aside, storing up as he may prosper, that there be no collections when I come." They were to give regularly, proportionally, happily, and sacrificially.

Some see 2 Corinthians 8:5 as an example of Christian tithing, as it addresses believers giving first to the Lord, then to Paul and his fellow missionaries. However, the verse mentions no specific amount, so it is not clear if Paul refers to a tithe or to giving in general.

It appears that the overall focus of the New Testament is not on a set amount but on generous and abundant giving to meet the needs of the church. The tithe is a historic precedent that can serve as a great example for church giving, but we have no biblical requirement to give an exact amount. Early believers gave much more at times, offering a pattern for those who are able to give more today.

Rather than focusing on an exact percentage, we should make every effort to financially support our local church and those who lead it, to generously give to missionaries who take the gospel to others, and to meet the needs of our family and of people in need as the Lord allows.

91. What does the Bible say about drinking alcohol? Is it a sin?

Should a Christian drink alcohol? This long-time question has been the source of much controversy among believers and for good reason. The misuse of alcohol has led to the destruction of many lives, whether through drunk driving, alcoholism, related health illnesses, or the relationships destroyed through its influence.

The Bible offers an interesting approach when it comes to whether a Christian can or should consume alcohol. First, Scripture teaches that we are to abide by the laws of our society. Romans 13:1 says, "Let every soul be subject to the governing authorities. For there is no authority except from God, and the authorities that exist are appointed by God."

Applied to the US, this means no one under the age of twenty-one should drink alcohol. There are also other laws prohibiting drinking and driving, banning alcohol in certain locations, and limiting how much alcohol can be consumed. Christians are, at a minimum, required to follow society's laws regarding alcohol usage.

Second, the Bible was written before modern refrigeration. An honest look at Scripture reveals that societies regularly consumed alcohol as part of the cultural norm. This largely included drinking wine, with even Jesus turning water into wine during a wedding as his first miracle (John 2:1–12). It would be difficult to draw the conclusion that God always forbids alcohol when it was included among the miracles Christ performed. Jesus also certainly drank wine during Passover and probably at other times as part of a normal meal.

Third, Scripture includes many warnings against the misuse of alcohol. In the New Testament, Paul told believers they were not to get drunk on wine but rather to be controlled by the Holy Spirit (Ephesians 5:18). The Bible clearly condemns drinking to the point of drunkenness.

Fourth, alcohol can lead a person astray. Proverbs 20:1 states, "Wine is a mocker, strong drink is raging: and whosoever is deceived thereby is not wise" (KJV). Scripture advised the use of wine and strong drink only for those who wanted to forget life and their misery:

> It is not for kings, O Lemuel,
> it is not for kings to drink wine,
> nor for princes intoxicating drink;
> lest they drink and forget the law,
> and pervert the justice of all the afflicted.
> Give strong drink to him who is perishing,
> and wine to those who are bitter of heart.
> Let him drink and forget his poverty,
> and remember his misery no more. (Proverbs 31:4–7)

Proverbs 23:31–33 also describes some of the ways alcohol can change our personality in negative ways:

> Do not look on the wine when it is red,
> when it sparkles in the cup,
> when it swirls around smoothly;
> at the last it bites like a serpent,
> and stings like a viper.
> Your eyes will see strange things,
> and your heart will utter perverse things.

Fifth, some people in the Bible chose not to drink wine or any form of alcohol to better serve the Lord. Some people also chose to abstain from strong drink for a period of time. This was called a Nazarite vow (Numbers 6). To make certain that he consumed no alcohol, the person under the vow also did not eat grapes or raisins.

Sixth, church leaders should be "not given to wine" (1 Timothy 3:3, 8; Titus 1:7). This doesn't fully prohibit the use of alcohol since wine was commonly used during communion. However, clearly, a church leader is not to consume much alcohol. Paul advised Timothy, a young leader in the church, to have some wine to help with his illness, which likely means he otherwise did not drink any wine (5:23).

An overall look at Scripture shows that God's Word does not fully ban the use of alcohol but rather provides several guidelines and warnings regarding its consumption. The easiest way to avoid the problems associated with alcohol in our time is to abstain from it completely, a choice we strongly recommend. Unlike biblical times when few other options existed for beverages, we have plenty of other choices that can help us focus our attention on God and serving others.

92. What does the Bible say about gambling?

Gambling, sports betting, casinos, and lottery tickets have become a major part of our culture over the past generation. Many advertisements claim the activities are harmless fun and can add to our income. Others argue that all forms of gambling are evil. What does the Bible say?

Scripture does not provide a direct verse that prohibits gambling, but it does have a lot to say about how believers are to invest their time and money. Gambling is largely negative for Christians because it takes a person's focus from using income to serve God and includes it in a high-risk attempt to make more money.

These types of activity can reveal a person's heart as having a love for money, an activity the Bible does condemn. "The love of money is a root of all kinds of evil, for which some have strayed from the faith in their greediness, and pierced themselves through with many sorrows," 1 Timothy 6:10 teaches. Hebrews 13:5 also warns against this love of money: "Let your conduct be without covetousness; be content with such things as you have. For He Himself has said, 'I will never leave you nor forsake you.'" God wants us to find our trust in him, not in our wealth or the pursuit of it.

In Matthew 6:24, Jesus warned against serving two masters, God and "mammon," a word other Bible versions translate as "money": "No one can serve two masters; for either he will hate the one and love the other, or else he will be loyal to the one and despise the other. You cannot serve God and mammon." People who pursue financial gain through gambling or betting also tend to rely on chance or luck, forgetting that the Lord controls all things. There is no such thing as luck in the Christian worldview. In Proverbs 16:33, Scripture teaches, "The lot is cast into the lap, but its every decision is from the LORD."

God clearly warns against a love of money and relying on chance to earn income. Considering these biblical teachings, we do not recommend any involvement in gambling, betting, or even purchasing lottery tickets. In addition, some forms of gambling involve large commitments of time that may take away from serving God in other areas. Sports betting, for example, has its own websites and programs that consume hours each week for some people who should be investing the same time in more godly activities.

However, Scripture does allow some freedom in this area. There have certainly been some occasions in which God has used a game of chance to allow someone to win in order to honor the Lord. Only God fully knows your heart and whether you are pursuing an activity to honor him.

In summary, we personally advise against any involvement in gambling. The Bible offers guidelines that warn about many aspects of betting money but does not outright condemn the practice. Those who choose to participate must do so wisely in order to avoid a love of money, misuse of time, and any large loss of financial resources that would better be used to care for godly needs.

SECTION 12

QUESTIONS ABOUT THE END TIMES

93. WHAT HAPPENS AFTER WE DIE?

The Bible speaks of heaven and hell in the afterlife, but what happens after we die? Scripture offers some details to help us better understand what to expect after we breathe our final breath in this world.

First, Scripture is clear that there is one life followed by a judgment. Hebrews 9:27 says, "As it is appointed for men to die once, but after this the judgment." The Bible does not allow for reincarnation, nor does it suggest that our life merely ends after this life.

Second, the Bible indicates a person will immediately be with the Lord or eternally separated from him. Paul wrote in Philippians 1:21, "For to me, to live is Christ, and to die is gain," adding in verse 23 that being with Christ "is far better." The apostle expressed the perspective that the believer immediately enters the presence of the Lord after death.

Paul also spoke of this reality in 2 Corinthians 5:6–8: "Therefore we are always confident, knowing that, whilst we are at home in the body, we are absent from the Lord: (For we walk by faith, not by sight:) We are confident, I say, and willing rather to be absent from the body, and to be present with the Lord" (KJV). There is no space for the concept of soul sleep (that our soul will "sleep" until Christ returns) or even for purgatory (a Catholic teaching that includes a third realm between heaven and hell).

Jesus gave evidence of this immediate experience in two places. In Luke 23:43, he told the repentant thief on the cross, "Assuredly, I say to you, today you will be with Me in Paradise." Both Jesus and the believing man would be in heaven that day.

The Lord also provided clarity on this issue in Luke 16:19–31. Lazarus died and was immediately at Abraham's side, a reference for heaven. The rich man, who was an unbeliever, was immediately in torment in hell. The destinations were also permanent, with no ability to move from hell to heaven (v. 26).

One major change is that our body will cease, but our spirit and soul will continue. Jesus taught in Matthew 10:28, "Do not fear those who kill the body but cannot kill the soul. But rather fear Him who is able to destroy both soul and body in hell." He added in John 11:26, "And whoever lives and believes in Me shall never die."

Ultimately, all people will dwell in a new heaven and new earth with the Lord or will be separated from him forever. "Anyone not found written in the Book of Life was cast into the lake of fire," Revelation 20:15 teaches regarding the unbeliever.

The believer, however, will experience the eternal presence of the Lord: "There shall be no more curse, but the throne of God and of the Lamb shall be in it, and His servants shall serve Him. They shall see His face, and His name shall be on their foreheads. There shall be no night there: They need no lamp nor light of the sun, for the Lord God gives them light. And they shall reign forever and ever" (22:3–5).

94. DOES THE BIBLE TEACH THAT WE ARE LIVING IN THE LAST DAYS?

The Bible claims we are certainly living in the last days, but it has also spoken of believers living in the last days since the time of the apostles. We are called to live with both an urgency that Jesus will return at any moment and to invest in each day to best serve the Lord where he has called us.

In Joel 2:28-29, the prophet predicted that an outpouring of the Holy Spirit would occur in the last days. This occurred during the day of Pentecost in Acts 2. Jesus also predicted that the Jewish temple would be destroyed in the last days, something that took place in AD 70 (Matthew 24).

Many aspects of the last days, however, seem to be unfolding more in our recent times. These signs include both negative and positive aspects. In 2 Timothy 3:1-5, Paul warned of the traits of people in the last days that seem to resemble many in the world today: "Know this, that in the last days perilous times will come: For men will be lovers of themselves, lovers of money, boasters, proud, blasphemers, disobedient to parents, unthankful, unholy, unloving, unforgiving, slanderers, without self-control, brutal, despisers of good, traitors, headstrong, haughty, lovers of pleasure rather than lovers of God, having a form of godliness but denying its power. And from such people turn away!"

Matthew 24:5-8 also adds to the list of predictions from Jesus regarding the last days: "Many will come in My name, saying, 'I am the Christ,' and will deceive many. And you will hear of wars and rumors of wars. See that you are not troubled; for all these things must come to pass, but the end is not yet. For nation will rise against nation, and kingdom against kingdom. And there will be famines, pestilences, and earthquakes in various places. All these are the beginning of sorrows." Global conflicts, famines, natural disasters, and more all appear to point to Christ coming soon.

Other fulfillments of the descriptions of the last days found in Daniel and Revelation seem to connect with modern technology. The mark of the beast, global communications, and world commerce (Revelation 13) all appear to closely fit the information age in which we now live that will identify as the culture during which a future Antichrist reigns. These aspects, combined with an increase in globalization, have led to many discussions regarding the last days.

However, not all "last days" descriptions are negative in the Bible. For example, the Bible predicts Israel ruling as a nation again in the last days (Ezekiel 37). Many last days' prophecies refer to Israel as a nation. The nation of Israel fell in AD 70 and was not a country for nineteen hundred years. In 1948, Israel became a nation again following World War II. Today it is one of the highest-ranked nations in the world in many key categories, with millions of Jews returning to the land over the past generation.

Matthew 24:14 predicts, "This gospel of the kingdom will be preached in all the world as a witness to all the nations, and then the end will come." Some see this prophecy unfolding today as Christians take the gospel to the last people groups who have not heard the good news, the Bible is translated into more languages, and technology is bringing Scripture and the gospel message to every part of the earth.

Some have grown discouraged at what seems like Christ's long time in waiting to return. However, Scripture offers a powerful reason for this: "The Lord is not slack concerning His promise, as some count slackness, but is longsuffering toward us, not willing that any should perish but that all should come to repentance" (2 Peter 3:9).

God's patience allows us to share the gospel with more people. We should be thankful for every moment and every day we have to share his message with others in these last days before his return.

95. DO OUR PETS GO TO HEAVEN?

Scripture is clear that there will be animals in heaven, but it leaves the discussion uncertain regarding whether our earthly pets will be there. Many animal lovers have asked us over the years whether they can expect to see their favorite dog, cat, or other pets in eternity with the Lord. A close look at the Bible offers it as a possibility but not as a certainty.

The most direct biblical passage related to this issue is found in Ecclesiastes 3:21. After speaking about issues of life and death, the author asked, "Who knows whether the spirit of man goes upward and the spirit of the beast goes down into the earth?" (ESV). Even King Solomon, considered the world's wisest man of his time, was uncertain whether animals go to heaven after death or whether they simply pass away.

Some argue that the clear distinction between animals and humans in Genesis 1–2 shows that humans will experience the afterlife but that animals will not. Unlike animal life, "the LORD God formed man of the dust of the ground, and breathed into his nostrils the breath of life; and man became a living being" (Genesis 2:7).

In addition, unlike animals, humans were created in the image of God: "Then God said, 'Let Us make man in Our image, according to Our likeness; let them have dominion over the fish of the sea, over the birds of the air, and over the cattle, over all the earth and over every creeping thing that creeps on the earth.' So God created man in His own image; in the image of God He created him; male and female He created them" (Genesis 1:26–27).

These distinctions do point to important differences between humans and animal life, but they do not rule out the possibility that animals will be in heaven. In fact, the Bible directly mentions animals in the afterlife. The millennial kingdom speaks of the wolf and the lamb dwelling together in peace (Isaiah 11:6; 65:25). The new heavens and new earth will include a completely different environment that could include many animals that may be the same or similar to animals now on earth (Revelation 21:1).

In addition, horses of fire took Elijah up to heaven (2 Kings 2:11). When Jesus returns, he will come riding a white horse (Revelation 19:11). Others will also follow him on white horses (Revelation 19:14).

God created animal life and certainly cares for his created beings. Jesus taught that the Lord knows and cares for every bird: "Look at the birds of the air, for they neither sow nor reap nor gather into barns; yet your heavenly Father feeds them" (Matthew 6:26).

The major aspect that we do not know is whether the same animals from earth will exist in heaven. The Bible does not provide an example of an animal from our world going to heaven. Though it is possible according to Scripture, we should not tell our children or others that pets will definitely go to heaven. Instead, we can rest assured that God has a perfect eternity in store for those who believe and that he will take care of all of his creation, including our beloved pets, according to his perfect will.

96. WHAT IS THE IMPORTANCE OF EZEKIEL 38 IN THE END TIMES?

Ezekiel 38 is often discussed in relation to unfulfilled Bible prophecy. It is the focus of many end-time books, conferences, and online articles, including some of the most popular prophecy novels and films of our time. Why is this chapter so important?

There are several reasons Ezekiel 38 is important regarding Bible prophecy, but the top reason is that it includes a variety of important surrounding nations attacking Israel. Verses 2-6 note several kingdoms that will lead

QUESTIONS ABOUT THE END TIMES ~ 201

their armies against Israel. A brief mention and likely modern equivalent of each nation is as follows:

- Magog, likely includes parts of Central Asia such as Kazakhstan, Kyrgyzstan, Uzbekistan, Turkmenistan, and Tajikistan. Some also include Afghanistan in this group. (Note: Gog is listed as the leader of this group of nations rather than as a nation in the group.)
- Rosh, likely Russia or at least part of it
- Meshech, part of modern Türkiye
- Tubal, part of modern Türkiye
- Persia, modern Iran
- Ethiopia, modern Sudan rather than modern Ethiopia
- Libya, modern Libya, also called Put in some translations
- Gomer, part of modern Türkiye
- Togarmah, part of modern Türkiye

Other nations may be involved, but Ezekiel specifically mentions the listed groups. These nations will come to war against Israel during a time of peace in Israel ("unwalled villages" in v. 11). In addition, verse 13 mentions "Sheba, Dedan, the merchants of Tarshish, and all their young lions." These nations include the Arabian Peninsula. They will oppose the battle but not intervene. Some believe the "young lions" refer to the areas to the west of Israel and the Middle East that would include Western European powers, the Americas, and Commonwealth nations, though this is uncertain. The Lord will supernaturally defeat the nations who oppose Israel, according to verses 18–23.

This future battle will likely occur during the seven-year tribulation described in Daniel and Revelation. Why? Because Israel will be under a peace agreement with the

Antichrist and the defeat will be followed by a great earthquake in Israel that appears to match the earthquakes in Revelation, perhaps occurring near the midpoint of the tribulation in association with the earthquake in Jerusalem in Revelation 11:13–19.

Another interesting aspect of Ezekiel 38 is that it describes Israel as an existing nation. Israel was reestablished as a nation in 1948 after nineteen hundred years. A portion of this prophecy has already, therefore, been fulfilled, and other aspects, such as certain nations already being in conflict with Israel, have also happened.

Though this prophecy is likely speaking of a time that will take place after the rapture and during the tribulation, its words remind us of God's promises to Israel, his plans for the future, and the importance of being prepared today regardless of the events taking place around us.

97. What does the Bible mean when it mentions a third heaven?

The Bible discusses a third heaven in 2 Corinthians 12:2–4. Paul described going there in a vision fourteen years before his letter to the Corinthian Christians. What is this third heaven?

In this passage, Paul wrote, "I know a man in Christ who fourteen years ago—whether in the body I do not know, or whether out of the body I do not know, God knows—such a one was caught up to the third heaven. And I know such a man—whether in the body or out of the body I do not know, God knows—how he was caught up into Paradise and heard inexpressible words, which it is not lawful for a man to utter."

The key to understanding the identity of the third heaven is to know how the Bible and the ancient world discussed heaven. Heaven and sky were translated from the same Greek word. The first heaven referred to the sky. We can also find this in the Old Testament, for example, with Deuteronomy 11:11 referring to rain falling from heaven. The Psalms and Prophets also refer to the sky as heaven (see, for example, Psalm 104:12; Isaiah 55:10).

The second heaven was outer space. This was the realm where the stars, moon, sun, and other planets dwell. For example, Isaiah 13:10 says, "For the stars of heaven and their constellations will not give their light; the sun will be darkened in its going forth, and the moon will not cause its light to shine."

The third heaven Paul mentioned in 2 Corinthians 12 is a reference to heaven, the location where the Lord dwells with believers who have passed away. Paul was uncertain whether he was there in a vision or for real, but he heard words he was not to repeat.

It is important to note that this third heaven is much different than the claimed "levels" of heaven suggested in fiction or by some other religious groups. For example, Dante's *Divine Comedy* suggests nine levels of heaven. Other religious movements claim various levels in the afterlife as well. For example, Jehovah's Witnesses have both a general paradise for faithful believers and a special level for the most holy and faithful 144,000 witnesses. The Church of Jesus Christ of Latter-day Saints teaches that three levels of the afterlife exist. They include the celestial, terrestrial, and telestial kingdoms. Mormon teachings claim the celestial kingdom is the same as the Bible's third heaven and that top Mormons and young children who die are the ones who reach this level. The Bible does not include this teaching.

The Bible does teach that there will be a new heaven and new earth at the end of time. Revelation 21–22 discusses the details regarding this location God will create after making all things new. It is important to note that this new heaven is an entirely different reality God will create.

It is not a third heaven that somehow follows two other evolutions of heaven.

The idea of a third heaven may sound odd in our culture, but Paul clearly used the term to distinguish the place in his vision from the sky and outer space, offering a visionary look at the eternal home of believers.

98. WHAT IS THE NEW JERUSALEM?

The New Jerusalem is the future eternal heavenly city God will create at the end of time. It will exist alongside the new heaven and new earth described in Revelation 21–22, the final two chapters of the Bible.

Revelation 21:9–27 offers a lengthy description regarding some of the beautiful aspects of this eternal city. First, the city will come out of the sky or heaven directly from the Lord: "He carried me away in the Spirit to a great and high mountain, and showed me the great city, the holy Jerusalem, descending out of heaven from God" (v. 10).

Verses 11–13 describe the twelve gates of the city: "Her light was like a most precious stone, like a jasper stone, clear as crystal. Also she had a great and high wall with twelve gates, and twelve angels at the gates, and names written on them, which are the names of the twelve tribes of the children of Israel: three gates on the east, three gates on the north, three gates on the south, and three gates on the west."

Verse 14 notes the city's wall and foundations: "Now the wall of the city had twelve foundations, and on them were the names of the twelve apostles of the Lamb." The city will be "laid out as a square" (v. 16). The size will be enormous, equivalent to 1,380 miles in each direction (2,220 kilometers). The wall will be designed with twelve precious stones (vv. 18–20).

Verse 21 explains that the twelve gates will be made from twelve giant pearls: "The twelve gates were twelve pearls: each individual gate was of one pearl. And the street of the city was pure gold, like transparent glass."

Verses 22–27 describe the glory of the New Jerusalem. The city will have no temple because "the Lord God Almighty and the Lamb are its temple" (v. 22). There will also be no sun or moon, as God will be its light (v. 23). The gates will always be open, symbolizing the eternal peace that those who are saved will experience (v. 25).

God's people appear to be able to freely travel in and out of the city, as the amazing description of the New Jerusalem will serve as only one part of God's astonishing new heavens and earth. The description concludes with the reminder that nothing will enter the city that is sinful: "There shall by no means enter it anything that defiles, or causes an abomination or a lie, but only those who are written in the Lamb's Book of Life" (v. 27).

Earlier, Revelation 3:12 also mentions the New Jerusalem: "He who overcomes, I will make him a pillar in the temple of My God, and he shall go out no more. I will write on him the name of My God and the name of the city of My God, the New Jerusalem, which comes down out of heaven from My God. And I will write on him My new name." This promise to the faithful believers in ancient Philadelphia reminds us that all believers will one day share in this glorious eternal city.

The focus on the New Jerusalem would have been of great importance to Jewish believers in the first century. The city of Jerusalem had been destroyed in AD 70 despite Jews believing it would be their eternal capital. Revelation 21 reminds believers that God does have a New Jerusalem in store for his people that will be eternal, where sin will no longer enter, and where God's people will forever dwell with him.

99. WILL THERE REALLY BE STREETS OF GOLD IN HEAVEN?

Many people say that the streets in heaven will be paved with gold. Is this true? If so, where does the Bible talk about these golden streets?

The origin of golden streets in heaven is found in the description of the New Jerusalem that will serve as part of the new heavens and earth described in Revelation 21–22. Revelation 21:21 says, "The street of the city was pure gold, like transparent glass." It does appear that at least this portion of eternity future includes golden streets, though we just keep in mind that the apostle John wrote based on his perception of the heavenly New Jerusalem. In other words, he described what he saw. Heaven may or may not have literal gold like on earth, but these roads will look like gold to those who are there.

What is the significance of golden streets that will exist at least in parts of heaven? First, the golden streets are part of the astounding description of the New Jerusalem that will be only one part of the future new heavens and earth where believers will dwell with God. In the time John wrote, the Romans had likely already destroyed Jerusalem. In contrast, the Lord will make all things new and improved in the end, putting an end to all shame, sadness, and destruction.

In addition to the streets of "pure gold," the description of the New Jerusalem also mentions gold two other times. In John's vision in verse 15, he measured aspects of the city with a gold reed or stick. In verse 18, the city itself was pure gold. It won't be only the streets. The entire city will shine with gold and other priceless materials. Verses 19–20 include twelve different precious stones: "The foundations of the wall of the city were adorned with all kinds of precious stones: the first foundation was jasper, the second sapphire, the third chalcedony, the fourth emerald, the fifth sardonyx, the sixth sardius, the seventh chrysolite, the eighth beryl, the ninth topaz, the tenth chrysoprase, the eleventh jacinth, and the twelfth amethyst." Some have also noted that the most valuable items in our world will serve as construction materials in heaven. That's actually a great point! What we consider of great worth on earth will be common in heaven. We will appreciate the beauty, but our focus will instead be on the Lord and the splendor of his majesty.

The beauty of eternity future is also designed to cause us to long for heaven. John concludes the book of Revelation by urging the Lord to fulfill his plans, saying, "Come, Lord Jesus!" (22:20). Verse 14 adds, "Blessed are those who do His commandments, that they may have the right to the tree of life, and may enter through the gates into the city." The Lord promises that his believers will one day enter this eternal city and walk on streets with the appearance of gold.

The greatness of heaven should also challenge us to share our faith with those who do not know God. Not only will unbelievers be excluded from eternity with the Lord and other believers, but they will also experience eternal judgment. Revelation 22:15 says unbelievers will be outside of this great eternal city: "Outside are dogs and sorcerers and sexually immoral and murderers and idolaters, and whoever loves and practices a lie." Revelation 20:15 adds that unbelievers will be eternally "cast into the lake of fire."

100. WHAT ARE THE NEW HEAVENS AND NEW EARTH?

The new heavens and earth are the eternal dwelling place of all believers described in Revelation 21–22, the final two chapters of the Bible. A brief look at these chapters reveals Christians have much to look forward to regarding our future home.

Revelation 21:1 begins with the words, "I saw a new heaven and a new earth, for the first heaven and the first earth had passed away. Also there was no more sea." The new heavens and earth will replace the former universe. This future state will also include a New Jerusalem, God's future heavenly city (v. 2), described in verses 9–27.

Chapter 22 includes a description of the river of life: "He showed me a pure river of water of life, clear as crystal, proceeding from the throne of God and of the Lamb. In the middle of its street, and on either side of the river, was the tree of life, which bore twelve fruits, each tree yielding its fruit every month. The leaves of the tree were for the healing of the nations" (vv. 1–2). The river will come directly from the throne of God, completing the perfect conditions for our heavenly home.

Verse 3 adds that the curse of sin will be broken. What Satan began through the serpent in Genesis 3 will end in God's new creation: "There shall be no more curse, but the throne of God and of the Lamb shall be in it, and His servants shall serve Him."

Verses 4–5 describe the reality of believers living forever in the presence of the Lord, with no darkness, reigning together with the Lord forever: "They shall see His face, and His name shall be on their foreheads. There shall be no night there: They need no lamp nor light of the sun, for the Lord God gives them light. And they shall reign forever and ever."

In the Old Testament, Isaiah also mentions the new heavens and earth: "For behold, I create new heavens and a new earth; and the former shall not be remembered or come to mind" (65:17). Isaiah 66:22 adds, "'For as the new heavens and the new earth which I will make shall remain before Me,' says the Lord, 'So shall your descendants and your name remain.'"

However, not every person will dwell with God in this future eternal home. Revelation 20:15 expresses the judgment unbelievers will experience for eternity apart from the Lord: "Whosoever was not found written in the book of life was cast into the lake of fire" (KJV). These words remind us that we must choose to follow the Lord by faith in this life. We are also called to make disciples of all nations (Matthew 28:18–20).

Peter taught how we are to respond to God's future plans regarding the new heavens and earth: "Since all these things will be dissolved, what manner of persons ought you to be in holy conduct and godliness, looking for and hastening the coming of the day of God, because of which the heavens will be dissolved, being on fire, and the elements will melt with fervent heat? Nevertheless we, according to His promise, look for new heavens and a new earth in which righteousness dwells" (2 Peter 3:11–13). Our goal must be to live fully for the Lord, looking forward to the any-moment coming of the Lord and our future eternal home with Christ.

Verses 17–18 also warn that the knowledge of our eternal future in the new heavens and earth should keep us from stumbling into sin in this life: "You therefore, beloved, since you know this beforehand, beware lest you also fall from your own steadfastness, being led away with the error of the wicked; but grow in the grace and knowledge of our Lord and Savior Jesus Christ."

THE ULTIMATE QUESTION: DO YOU KNOW FOR SURE YOU ARE GOING TO HEAVEN?

People everywhere invest their lives in the search for meaning, purpose, and fulfillment. But people need something more than money, fame, luxurious houses, good looks, nice cars, or a lucrative stock portfolio. There is nothing necessarily wrong with these things, but they cannot provide peace to the soul or forgiveness of one's sin.

I once read that the highest rates of suicide and divorce occur among the most affluent classes of society. On the West Coast, psychologists and counselors have isolated a new affliction and given it a name, "sudden wealth syndrome." People are achieving every benchmark that our society says should make them happy, but they are finding that it is possible to be materially rich yet spiritually bankrupt. Many people have a schedule that is full but a heart that is empty.

In our daily live broadcast, *Exploring the Word*, we have had conversations with countless people who wrestle with probing questions and genuine concern about spiritual issues. People today truly are looking for meaningful answers, craving hope in a dangerous world.

Present realities, such as worldwide terrorist attacks, global economic uncertainty, political instability, natural disasters like Hurricane Ian, and COVID-19, have only intensified this search. Daily, we are honored to speak to people across America and internationally. They hear our shows, call us during the Q and A portions of our program, and send us emails and letters. These valued listeners may each express themselves in different ways, but they all have the same basic question:

WHO IS GOD, AND HOW MAY I COME TO KNOW HIM?

Where one stands with God is the most vital of all issues, but the good news is that you may settle this today. You may have wondered, *How does a person become a Christian? How can I be certain that my sin is forgiven? How may I experience consistent spiritual growth?* Let's consider these things together.

GOD'S WORD EXPLAINS THE MESSAGE OF SALVATION

Jesus said in John 3:3, "No one can see the kingdom of God unless they are born again" (NIV). Salvation is the issue. The most important question you will ever ask yourself is this: *Do I know for certain that I have eternal life and that I will go to heaven when I die?*

If you stood before God right now and God asked, "Why should I let you into my heaven?" what would you say?

The Bible describes our condition: "All have sinned and fall short of the glory of God" (Romans 3:23 NIV). Just as a job pays a wage at the end of the week, our sins will yield a result at the end of a lifetime: "The wages of sin is death [the Bible describes this as separation from God, the punishment of hell], but the gift of God is eternal life in Christ Jesus our Lord" (6:23 NIV).

> God's love for you personally is shown by His provision for your need: "But God demonstrated His love toward us, in that while we were yet sinners, Christ died for us" (Romans 5:8 [paraphrase]).
>
> Salvation requires repentance, which means a "turning." Jesus said, "Unless you repent, you will all likewise perish" (Luke 13:3 [ESV]). The New Testament emphasizes the necessity of repentance and salvation: "Repent therefore and be converted, that your sins may be blotted out" (Acts 3:19).
>
> Every one of us has sinned, and the Bible says that our sins must be dealt with. We have a two-fold sin problem. We are sinners by birth, and we are sinners by choice. Someone once spoke with the great evangelist Dr. Vance Havner, "This thing about man's sin nature, I find that hard to swallow!" Dr. Havner said, "You don't have to swallow it—you're born with it; it's already in you."
>
> The world classifies sin, viewing some things as worse than others. But the Bible teaches that all sin

is an offense against God, and even one sin is serious enough to keep someone out of heaven. You may not have robbed a bank, or maybe you have. God doesn't grade on a curve; humanity is a tainted race, and sin is the problem.

Oftentimes in life, we know what is right, but we do what is wrong. You may have even looked back at yourself and wondered, "What was I thinking? Why did I do that? How could I have said that?" Jesus said that man needs to repent, and make a change. Repentance means turning from your sins, and to Christ. By faith, trust who Jesus is (God's Son; mankind's Savior), and what Jesus did (died in your place, and rose from the dead). God's forgiveness is received by faith. We are to confess our faith before others, not ashamed to let the world know that we believe in Jesus: "That if you confess with your mouth the Lord Jesus and believe in your heart that God has raised Him from the dead, you will be saved. For with the heart one believes unto righteousness, and with the mouth confession is made unto salvation" (Romans 10:9–10).

What is faith? Faith is trust. It is simple, honest, child-like trust. God says that you have a sin problem, but that He loves you, and will forgive you. God says that through Jesus Christ, He has made a way for anyone to be saved who will come to Him. Do you trust what God has said, and what God has done? If you come to Christ in belief and faith, God promises to save you: "For whoever calls upon the name of the Lord, shall be saved" (v. 13 [paraphrase]). Jesus promises: "The one who comes to Me I will by no means cast out" (John 6:37).[9]

---

9 Alex McFarland, "God Loves You!," Southern Baptist Evangelists, accessed March 25, 2021, https://www.sbcevangelist.org/evangelists/everlasting-life/god-loves-you/.

In touring and speaking throughout all fifty states (and internationally), we have given away thousands of yellow stickers that read, "Jesus Saves, Pray Today!" That is not a trite saying or marketing cliché. It is a deep biblical truth, and if you desire to have a relationship with the Lord, you can accomplish that right where you are now. Make your journey to the cross today, through this basic prayer of commitment:

> *"Dear Lord Jesus, I know that I have sinned, and I cannot save myself. I believe that you are the Son of God, and that you died and rose again for me, to forgive my sins, and to be my Savior. I turn from my sins, and I ask you to forgive me. I receive you into my heart as my Lord and Savior. Jesus, thank you for saving me now. Help me to live the rest of my life for you. Amen."*[10]

GOD'S WORD GIVES YOU ASSURANCE OF SALVATION

You can overcome doubts about where you stand with God. Based on what God's Word says (not what you feel or assume), you can know that you have eternal life: "Whoever has the Son has life; whoever does not have the Son of God does not have life. I write these things to you who believe in the name of the Son of God so that you may know that you have eternal life" (1 John 5:12–13 NIV).

Jesus said, "Whoever hears my word and believes Him who sent me has eternal life and will not be judged but has crossed over from death to life" (John 5:24 NIV). Remember: you are not saved by good works, and you are not "kept saved" by good works. Your merit before God is totally based on Jesus; God credits his perfection, holiness, and righteousness to each one who believes by faith.

---

10 Alex McFarland, "God Loves You!"

WHAT DOES THE TERM *REDEDICATION* MEAN?

A news reporter once asked me this question. He had heard me use this term as I spoke at a church, and he wanted to know what I meant. *Rededication* is for a believer who desires to renew and deepen their walk with Christ. A Christian can wander from God in sin or simply lose their closeness to the Lord through the business of life.

A born-again Christian is forever God's child. Your salvation is a matter of sonship. Your daily Christian growth is a matter of fellowship. Your spiritual birth into God's family is, in some ways, similar to your physical birth into your human family. For instance, in growing up as a child, you may have disobeyed and disappointed your father. Something you did may have grieved your father, but you were still his child because you had been born into that family.

In the same way, the Christian's relationship to the Lord is still intact even though a sin we commit may hinder our daily fellowship with God. Salvation is a one-time, instantaneous event; Christian growth and personal fellowship with God is an everyday, lifelong process. Consistent daily prayer, Bible study, obedience to the Holy Spirit, and nurturing in a local church fellowship are all keys to growth and Christian maturity.

While your "sonship" may be intact, your daily "fellowship" may be lacking. Christ, not "self," must be on the throne of your heart and life. Sin hinders our fellowship with God. "Your iniquities have separated you from your God; your sins have hidden his face from you, so that he will not hear" (Isaiah 59:2 NIV). Perhaps your desire is like that of David, when he had wandered from God: "Create in me a pure heart, O God, and renew a steadfast spirit within me" (Psalm 51:10 NIV).

God lovingly receives all who turn to him and all who return to him. He cleanses us from sin and restores us to fellowship with him. King David had been "a man after

[God's] own heart" (1 Samuel 13:14 NIV), but his sinful deeds required that he humbly recommit himself to the Lord: "Do not cast me from your presence...Restore to me the joy of your salvation" (Psalm 51:11–12 NIV). Christian publications often use the following verse in the context of evangelism, and that is okay, but 1 John 1:9 is really a promise to the Christian who needs to make things right with the Lord: "If we confess our sins, he is faithful and just and will forgive us our sins and purify us from all unrighteousness" (NIV).

From the same chapter is another great truth that gives us precious, sweet assurance: "If we walk in the light, as he is in the light, we have fellowship with one another, and the blood of Jesus, his Son, purifies us from all sin" (v. 7 NIV).

You may already know the Lord but wish to pray these basic words of rededication and commitment:

*Lord Jesus, I acknowledge that I have
sinned and wandered from you. I confess
my sin and turn from it. I recommit myself
to you as Lord. Thank you for forgiving me; I
trust you to give me the strength to live for
you each day of my life. Thank you for being
my Savior, my Lord, and my friend. Amen.*

May God bless you as you journey on with him!

If you made a decision for Christ just now, we would be honored to hear from you. If you do not have a Bible and would like to request one or if you have other questions or spiritual needs, write to

Alex & Bert / *Exploring the Word*
c/o AFA Radio
PO Drawer 2440
Tupelo, MS 38803

You may email us with more questions or other comments at word@afr.net.

ABOUT THE AUTHORS

 **ALEX MCFARLAND** is an evangelist, author, and advocate for Christian apologetics. Cohost of *Exploring the Word* with Bert Harper (heard nationally on the American Family Radio Network), Alex is the founder of America's longest-running series of apologetic conferences, Truth for a New Generation. He has served as president of Southern Evangelical Seminary and director of Teen Apologetics for Focus on the Family under James Dobson. In addition to his work with the American Family Association, Alex directs Biblical Worldview for Charis Bible College. He has served as an adjunct professor at several Christian universities, assisting with the creation of programs and departments dedicated to apologetics and the defense of the Christian worldview. Alex is the author of many books, including the best-selling *10 Most Common Objections to Christianity.* He is a graduate of the Liberty University Graduate School of Religion. Alex and his wife, Angela, live in North Carolina.

BERT HARPER is the director of Marriage, Family, and Pastoral Ministries at the American Family Association. He has served as cohost of *Exploring the Word* with Alex McFarland for more than a decade and is heard on an average of two hundred stations nationwide each weekday afternoon. Bert Harper has nearly four decades of experience in the role of senior pastor, faithfully preaching God's Word, leading biblically and by example, and impacting countless lives for the gospel. He and his wife, Jan, have invested themselves in counseling couples and mentoring and helping families in full-time Christian ministry. Bert Harper has faithfully served on the board of the American Family Association and Blue Mountain College and in many other leadership roles on behalf of churches and Christian organizations. Together, he and Jan lead Fishbowl—an annual retreat for ministers and their wives. The Harpers have three grown sons and are the proud grandparents of a growing family.